DORSET INNS

DORSET INNS

Harry Ashley

With Illustrations by John Baker

COUNTRYSIDE BOOKS
NEWBURY, BERKSHIRE

First Published 1987
© Harry Ashley 1987

COUNTRYSIDE BOOKS
3 Catherine Road
Newbury, Berkshire

ISBN O 905392 83 3

Produced Through MRM (Print Consultants) Ltd., Reading
Printed in England

Dedication

To the 50 year old enriching memory of an elegant and beautiful
brunette in a North Dorset Gentlemen's Bar who, tending well lit
optics, reminded me of a High Priestess at an altar.

She talked to me of many things and held me in her spell, but I
never knew her name.

Foreword

The English inn is part of our heritage and you will not find its like anywhere in the world. I have supped thin French beer at quayside cafes in Cherbourg, and partaken of white wine and hard boiled eggs in Saigon. In the Chinese hill town of Kunming, acute sickness followed eggs boiled in clay, fifty years old, washed down with a Chinese style whisky. Cairo, and the famous but disappointing Shepherds Hotel, offered me gin based John Collins, well iced, and in Singapore I tasted the most depressing of all alcoholic drinks, Saki.

At Arab hotels I have enjoyed deceptively mild aniseed drinks and once, in a rest house on a lonely road in Sri Lanka, was arrested for signing the visitors' book as Hermann Goering. But nowhere in my travels have I found anything to equal the English pub, with cool beer and serving traditional bread and cheese lunches.

My grandmother contended that village life centred around the church, inn and baker's shop, but I never discovered the importance of the latter. No two inns are alike and there is a local county pride in beer quality. The harder bitters are favoured by northerners who dislike the sweeter ales of the south. The Yorkshireman boasts of Tadcaster ales brewed by the brothers Smith. In the Midlands the Burton brews are favoured, and here in the south we boast ale fit for agricultural men. Rail travellers going south-west out of London will remember the giant signs which stood in the fields. Against a background of rich farming downs, they proclaimed 'You are now in the Strong Country', referring to the Romsey brews. Further along the coast at Weymouth, the air carried the sweet aroma of malt and hops from the premises of the rival brewers Groves and Devenish. The Dorset county town is proud of Huntsman ale, and Eldridge Pope even brewed a special ale to celebrate Thomas Hardy's Centenary. Hall and Woodhouse, brewing in the Stour valley on the river's banks at Blandford, are internationally famous for their Badger Beers, and both the latter breweries have family members still in the businesses. At Bridport, Palmers Brewery still has the water wheel from which it once derived power from the River Brit, and young Palmers are still in charge. Sadly, Strong houses now carry the name Whitbread since the takeover of many breweries, and Groves and Devenish no longer brew at Weymouth.

There was a time when each inn had its own character and was presided over by the landlord running his pub the way he chose, and if he did not want your company, you were soon told. The system produced many amusing personalities, some whose names live long after they have passed on. Today the landlords are slowly being replaced by managers trained by the breweries, serving ale from canisters over which they have little control. Inns have given up the bread and cheese image and rival each other, catering wise, with choice menus and food specialities. Cosy bars for drinking are being replaced by larger rooms with more space devoted for eating. Sadly, many of the managers are catering specialists and often, if you ask them which beer they recommend, they will tell you that they do not drink the stuff.

At some time or other, the inn plays a part in our lives and we cherish personal memories of favourite hostelries. It may be a farewell party, or a reunion. It may be a wartime recollection of a village inn near a camp or aerodrome, and happy singsongs far into the night. It could even be a secret or treasured meeting with someone close. In my personal recollections, even murder plays a part. There was also a thatched inn by a stream where I entertained a fresh faced blonde a long time ago. As a child, I was brought up with cats and have an affinity for the feline creatures. They choose me out of a crowd and come purring to my lap. On this occasion, the pub cat shared the laps of my companion and myself as we sat by the open fire. 'A cat lover', I mused, and later married her only to find that she did not like cats and I have had to live my life with dogs.

This book tells of the inns of Dorset which I have known and used over 50 years. Some of them have now gone, but it will give the yonger reveller some idea of the character of the old inns before all the surviving ones have become restaurants to cater for the needs of a new generation.

It is not a guide to the best inns – there are many more excellent ones – but this is my story of hostelries which have played a part in my life, laced with anecdotes of cherished places that have given me pleasure.

Sometimes I have used the names of landlords or managers in the anecdotes but in an age when hosts frequently change there is no guarantee that you will find the named persons in those inns today.

Harry. W. Ashley

Sailors Return East Chaldon

Smiths Arms, Godmanstone

Introduction

The Old Boro' Arms at Weymouth stood atop a hill on the Chickerell road. You will not be able to drink there now – the building is used as a youth club – but it was here in the early 1920s that my story begins.

It was a very ordinary John Groves house, and had spittoons along the base of the bar and sawdust covered the wooden floor. Each evening, my old seafaring grandfather would put on his naval cap and set out for the inn a hundred yards down the road. He took with him a white jug to bring home a quart of stout for my grandmother. On summer evenings, I would be allowed to walk with him to the Old Boro' and wait outside until he was ready to return.

It was like Aladdin's cave. I wondered what was inside. What caused the laughter? Why did the lady who served the beer keep giggling, and why were some men singing loudly? As the doors opened and shut to allow customers to enter and leave, I edged forward to get a glimpse inside. Through the haze of tobacco smoke, the men chatted in groups. Once I saw my grandfather in conversation with the giggling lady who was leaning across the bar, her enormous bosom being flattened against it. There was a pungent aroma of beer and smoke.

My mother, who was very against 'strong drink', told me that the inn was an evil place and never to go inside. But secretly I knew that I could not wait for the day when I was old enough to enter and feel those doors swing behind me.

Oddly enough, I never did. When I had reached the drinking age I had moved away from the district. So the four ale bar of the Old Boro' Arms remains a mystery, but I have found the answers to my questions in many other Dorset inns.

THE ANCHOR
Seatown

*Turn off the A35 road at Chideock and
follow the road down to the beach.*

THE Chideock gang of smugglers in the 17th century, who with their leader 'The Colonel' operated a small section of the West Dorset beach between Seatown and Charmouth, had the magnificent Golden Cap – a 617 feet high cliff pinnacle – as their signal station.

The true identity of the Colonel was never discovered, but he was believed to have been a local Squire. One thing is certain, the smugglers frequently took refreshment at the *Anchor Inn* on the beach at Seatown, one of the most attractive little inns in Dorset and, incidentally, situated right on the Great Coastal Path.

The Anchor has a family room where children can be catered for, and in summer visitors can sit at tables outside on a terraced patio overlooking the West Bay. A local duo sometimes entertain.

The ale sold at the Anchor is brewed at the picturesque Bridport brewery of Palmers. It is a family concern, and two Palmers of a new generation run it today. The brewery was originally powered by a water wheel driven by the river Brit, and it can still be seen – but now it is only decoration.

A Palmers house.

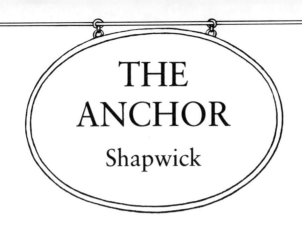

THE ANCHOR

Shapwick

In Shapwick village. Turn off the B3082 from Wimborne, half way along the famous tree avenue at Badbury Rings.

IF you think it odd that the inn at Shapwick, in the peaceful Stour valley, should be named The Anchor . . . it would not seem so strange if you came when the Dorset Stour overflows its banks and the whole of the village gets flooded up to the inn's door.

The village was the scene of a strange story many years ago, and you can read about the legend of the Shapwick crab on the walls of one of the bars in The Anchor. It seems that a fishmonger, passing through the village, mislaid a giant Portland crab and it had to be the village idiot who found it. He ran screaming through the streets. The local sage had taken to his bed many years before, but they wheeled him to the site in a wheelbarrow. He pronounced that it was a sea monster and bade everyone to keep away from it. The whole village felt silly when the fishmonger returned and picked the 'monster' up by its back.

The Anchor by the Cross is the only popular hostelry in the village, so do not be excited if you see the famous name of Picadilly, near the village centre. There are no night clubs, or theatres, in this quiet lane of cottages, with roses round the doors.

The Anchor has a beer garden and play place for children. It serves pub food and there is country and western singing on Thursdays, led by the landlord.

A Hall & Woodhouse inn.

13

The Barley Mow
Broomhill Wimborne

THE BARLEY MOW
Colehill

Colehill is just over a mile north west of Wimborne.

THE *Barley Mow* hides itself in the quiet lanes of Colehill. After 50 years I still get lost trying to find it. Once you are in the warmth of this cosy inn with its brick chimney corner, you will agree that the search was well worthwhile.

Some 600 years ago it was a drover's cottage and Cromwell's troops were billeted around it. In your search for the pub you will probably find Gods Blessing Lane. That is where Cromwell had his troops blessed before the battle for Corfe Castle.

The host describes the *Barley Mow* as being the last house in Colehill and it is situated in Long Lane, which is near Colehill Lane. To make it even more confusing, he says to follow the signs to Broomhill and you are quite near.

Best to come first time in daylight because it is a charming spot for a lunchtime drink and meal beneath shady umbrellas outside the inn. Here you can rest peacefully away from traffic and 'far from the madding crowd.'

A Hall & Woodhouse inn.

THE BLACK DOG
Weymouth

In St. Marys Street near the King's statue and seafront.

A LTHOUGH the *Black Dog* is Weymouth's oldest inn, its antiquity often goes unnoticed because it has become engulfed in St. Mary's Street edifices of later periods. The newer Georgian and Victorian facades cannot alter the fact that this was once a smugglers' haunt in the 16th century, and called the *Dove*. It became the *Black Dog* when the Master of a Newfoundland trading vessel gave the landlord a black labrador as a present. It was the first of the breed to enter the country.

The interior of this fine old inn is divided into bars around a central enclosed courtyard. Each bar is full of character but already there are plans afoot to modernise and rebuild the inn with larger bars. Until that happens, come and enjoy the old world charm and see the display on the walls of hundreds of naval cap bands recalling the names of battle craft over several decades, because in the days when Britain had a large Home Fleet, this was very much a sailor's pub. Amongst the fare that can be enjoyed is Portland Crab. During the last war, the roof of the *Black Dog* was used as base for a light machine gun post, in case the enemy approached via Weymouth Bay which the back of the inn overlooks.

The *Black Dog* had evil beginnings. When it stood alone on the sandy shore in the 16th century, it was the scene of two violent murders. In the 17th century, when the Civil War was raging in

Dorset, a guest who sought shelter there was murdered by the landlord, but no apparent reason can be found for the act. Later, in smuggling days, a Revenue Officer was cut down whilst attempting to arrest a smuggler at the inn.

On a more cheerful note, it is said that Daniel Defoe once stayed at the inn and worked on his famous book *Robinson Crusoe*.

A Devenish house.

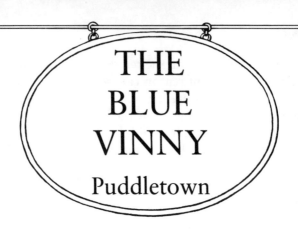

THE BLUE VINNY

Puddletown

Situated on the A354 near Puddletown traffic lights. Puddletown is on the main A35 road from Dorchester to Poole.

THE *Blue Vinny* inn carries the name of Dorset's illustrious cheese, but although the landlord may serve you portions of a cheese called Blue Vinny, it bears little resemblance to the taste of the original product . . . and that is no fault of those who claim to produce it today. The recipes are still in existence, but when the milk factories arrived, the original style cheese died. It appears that hand-skimmed milk was the secret. In the old days butter and cheese were made at the farms. Today, the milk is sold and is skimmed with mechanical separators before it is more than twelve hours old. This does not give the bacteria a chance to get into the cheese to turn it blue.

All manner of strange stratagems were used to give Blue Vinny its distinctive flavour. Some left the cheese to mature near a pair of old boots or horse's harness, believing that the leather acted as a conductor to guide the bacteria into the cheese. Others boiled the leaves of a sort of wild hollyhock and poured it in to make the cheese turn colour. Getting the cheese blue was the major problem.

Furthermore, the original Blue Vinny was a rough cheese, a filling lunch for agricultural workers and a very acquired taste. I remember Blue Vinny being set up on the bar of *The Greyhound Hotel* at Bridport by that famous pre-war host Walter Trump. The top was cut off the round cheese which had a rind like an

18

elephant's hide. Vinegar was poured in to soften it and customers dug a spoon into the cheese as they required it.

In the early 1970s Brian Jackman, a *Sunday Times* feature writer, made a county search for original Blue Vinny. Cheese authorities in London told him that cheese passed off as Blue Vinny nowadays is second-grade Stilton. He did not find his treasure but did unearth the long and complicated recipe copied out by a Powerstock woman in the 1920s, when she was a girl. 'Use the evening and morning's milk,' it began and ended: 'Should be kept 4 months at least to go blue'.

I fear it would not be viable to produce this cheese today, with a taste like Stilton although a lot drier, very crumbly and almost mildewed. (The word Vinny in Dorset dialect means mould or mildewed.) So to those who believe they are eating Blue Vinny, enjoy your milder Dorset Blue because you would probably not be able to stomach the original coarse Blue Vinny.

However, the inn stands as a memorial to the cheese. A place which welcomes children and has a family dining room. There is also a large garden.

A Devenish house.

THE BOOT INN

Weymouth

Situated in the old Weymouth High Street.
Over the Town Bridge and just to the right.

NOT far from the *Ship Inn* and just over the Town Bridge is
the location of the old Weymouth High Street, which
existed for centuries until a German land mine flattened it
during the Second World War. Had this not happened, I am sure
it would have been preserved as a precinct. Quaint old shops lined
each side of the narrow street. Two steps led you down into a
shoemaker's shop where Mr. Bonsor would measure your feet and
fit you out with a pair of handmade shoes for a few shillings. On
the other side, a gas-lit shop sold everything from wet fish to toys
and packets of needles. Behind were the stables which housed
Weymouth's famous beach donkeys. This street at night resembled
a scene from a Dickens novel, but it all went in one night of hatred
as German bombers passed óverhead.

Two of the old buildings survived. The Town Hall, originally
built in the 16th century, and the *Boot Inn,* an inn of character
where you still expect to see drunken pirates of the 17th century
come swaggering out with casks of ale on their shoulders. The
building has five light windows covered with hood moulds and
with hollow chamfered mullions. The name 'Boot' is derived from
nearby Boot Hill. In stagecoach days, the lowest fare paying
passengers rode outside the coach on the boot and were expected
to get off when it stopped at the inn, and help push it up the steep
hill.

Today it is a cosy hostelry where one customer told me you are
more likely to find a poacher than a pirate.

A Devenish house.

BRACE OF PHEASANTS

Plush

On the B3143 road from Dorchester. Turn right in Piddletrenthide.

WALKERS in the Piddle Valley near Dorchester climb the slopes which lead to Plush, peaceful village at the heart of Dorset, where the picturesque inn is constructed from two 16th century domestic dwellings and a forge. It became an inn in the mid 1930s, was renamed the Brace of Pheasants in 1957, and became a popular out of town eating house. In 1979 it was destroyed by fire but the listed building was restored and today is hosted by a young couple with experience in Bournemouth and Poole catering establishments.

This is a real family pub with lovely lawns and a rose garden, where the dogs are introduced as members of the welcoming team. Becky (the black one), Golden Lady is scallywag and Old Boy is George. You meet them all when you come to enjoy the fare at this free house, where game dishes are featured.

Nearby is the unique Dorset Orchid Farm.

A free house.

23

THE BRIDGE INN
Preston

Preston is on the A353 coast road about 4 miles out of Weymouth. Look for the Bridge Inn sign at the bottom of the hill.

THE Bridge Inn is on the banks of the river Jordan – not the famous one, but a stream at Preston near Weymouth. In fact Dorset's Jordan is scarcely deep enough to baptise a mouse. The 400 year old pub – obscured, but near the main Weymouth to Bournemouth coast road – is situated in a little community with its own village green. The inn was formerly called the *Swan* until 1936, but today resident ducks entertain those who choose to sit and drink in the beer garden.

The very large bar is unexpected – cosy and festooned with Christmas decorations on my last visit.

The hosts feature home cooking. Their two sons and daughter assist in running the family house.

The Bridge has gentle background music and, on some evenings in summer, barbecues are held on the green.

A pleasant spot, unknown by many Dorset folk who motor past daily, the inn has a children's room and a large patio is planned.

There are rumours of a ghost, but the landlady prefers not to talk about it.

A Devenish house.

THE BULL
Bridport

The hotel is situated at the centre of the town's shopping centre on the main east to west road

THE Dorset historian, Sir Frederick Treves, penned a beautiful description of Bridport. He said 'It is a homely county town, with an air about it of substantial simplicity. It has made no effort at history making, nor at the heaping up of annals.' How right he was, and in its languid part in the great Civil War it was sometimes held by the King and sometimes by Parliament, nobody really caring who was in charge.

But on June 13th 1685 Bridport was 'surprised' by the arrival of 300 of Monmouth's men under Lord Grey, and there was an unfortunate fracas at the *Bull Inn*. Although the full circumstances are obscure, it would seem that Colonel Edward Coker of Mappowder was killed on a staircase by the rebels. It is recorded in the parish church records that Col. Edward Coker, son of Captain Robert Coker of Mappowder, was slain at the *Bull Inn* on June 14th 1685 by one Venner, who was an officer under the late Duke of Monmouth in that Rebellion.

An unconfirmed story tells of a German U-Boat Commander who surfaced off West Bay in the last war and came ashore, made his way to the Bull where he had an enjoyable evening, dined well and then returned unrecognised to his ship. Said one local with similar thinking to Treves: 'If he had done it today, he would probably have got a parking ticket.'

A free house.

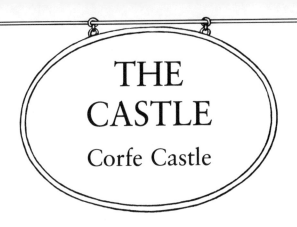

THE CASTLE
Corfe Castle

On the main road out of Corfe toward Swanage. A351.

WHO is Miss Colley, who haunts the *Castle Inn* at Corfe Castle? Much of the 300 year old inn was disturbed during refurbishment by landlord, Trevor Thomas, and two open fireplaces – one with a rare wood burner – have been exposed. Trevor's three year old son, Daniel, says he has talked to a lady in the bar called Miss Colley and 'she wears tall clothes.'

Trevor's wife, Pat, has also seen the ghost in a bedroom asking the way out, but Trevor says if he meets the ghost he will leave the house. Trevor, who left the Purbecks to serve eight years in the Somerset Police Force, returned to follow his father as Mine Host of this cosy little inn, which was the scene of the swordfight in Thomas Hardy's tale The Hand of Ethelberta.

It has an attractive new inn sign depicting the Castle but the old sign, now hanging on the bar wall, is far more interesting. It depicts the moment of murder in Corfe Castle when young King Edward was got rid of by his stepmother, the jealous Queen Elfrida in AD 978. She is seen holding the horse's head as a servant plunges the dagger into Edward's back.

Lunch and evening meals are served and the inn sometimes has folk singers in the bar.

There is also a beer garden and a large car park at this inn situated on the main road toward Swanage.

A Whitbread house.

THE CASTLE TAVERN

Christchurch

Situated in the heart of Christchurch on the approach road to the Priory.

THE *Castle Tavern* is very much part of the ancient history of Christchurch. It was built as a residence in 1660 in what was the moat of the Castle. The stronghold had been made a ruin ten years before, after bitter battles had been fought over the sacred ground of the Priory town between Royalists and Roundheads. The tavern still boasts a Norman wall as part of the kitchen.

This friendly tavern is now a free house and on Wednesdays visitors can enjoy folk music in the bar.

Popular star of the tavern is Molly the cook who organises set specials each day.

The Castle Tavern has a character functions room in which up to 90 guests can be catered for.

In 1645, Lord Goring held Christchurch for the royalists in the Civil War, the Roundheads holding the Castle and Priory. Goring withdrew fearing Roundhead reinforcements.

The inn specialises in real ales including some with interesting names like Fortyniner – a rich tasting strong ale – and Old Thumper, a very strong prize winning ale described as a good medicine.

A free house.

THE COACH & HORSES
Wimborne

Situated on the main road as it enters
Wimborne from Poole.

THE thatched cottage which forms the frontage of the *Coach & Horses* at Wimborne was built in the 15th century, but it is uncertain when it became a public house.

We do know that the *Coach* had a well-known character as its landlord before the Second World War. Jovial George Wentworth was installed there when he gave up his position as coachman to Lord Wimborne, whose residence was the building we know as Canford School.

Older drinkers will remember the sign 'YER TIZ' painted on the outside gents' toilet, adjacent to the main road. Emerging on a dark night, you stood the chance of that visit being your last act on earth if a passing car came too close.

The popular inn has been enlarged and the hosts serve hot and cold meals at the bar. The inn preserves its traditional pub image, but it is very different from the bars where our school of journalists met each week before the Second World War, on the home patch of a portly, bucolic character who was a farming correspondent. We used to sit on hard benches and listen with glee to the amusing bickering of George Wentworth and his fiery lady wife.

I must recall one of the volume of anecodotes remembered from the *Coach*.

Our Wimborne colleague would be known to imbibe about 20 pints a day, and to reach his home safely he would cross the main road from the *Coach*, find the gatepost and count a specific number of railings, then cross the road again and he would be opposite his own gate. One night he miscounted and started to crawl upstairs at the house next door. It was the home of a police officer.

A Whitbread house.

COVE INN

Chiswell – Portland

Drive along Chiswell from Portland Square.
The Cove Inn is high on the beach to your
right.

THE *Cove Inn* at Chiswell has been the centre of shipwrecks and drama all through its existence. No wonder, with its foundations built into the pebbles of Chesil Beach at the eastern end of West Bay, the infamous Channel waters which Thomas Hardy described as 'Deadmans Bay, where bones of thousands are.' Here in summer as a gentle sea swell fondles the pebbles, the fishermen of Portland pull ashore the loaded nets full of the world famous Portland mackerel. To protect Chiswell from the winter gales which sometimes roar over the beach bringing sea water to flood the Square, an elaborate defence system with flood gates has been constructed and the *Cove* is built into the complex, like a miniature stone fortress.

If you are a romantic with a sense of adventrue, this is the pub for you. It serves meals only at lunchtime, and there are no prizes for guessing that the specialities of the house are mackerel and the island's giant crabs.

The *Cove* has been in existence since 1887 and, for much of its history, was hosted by Combens and Saunders, both well-known families on this little isle. Today's landlords are 'foreigners' (not from a Portland family). This would have been unheard of 50 years ago, and is some proof that the island is losing its prejudices and insularity.

The windows of the *Cove* give panoramic views of the Portland cliff coast and the famous Chesil Beach which extends to Bridport. As you sup your ale, remember the countless seamen who have been carried into the bar exhausted after shipwreck. The inn remembers its exciting past with one bar which commemorates the ships literally wrecked on the doorstep. Photographs show the *Patric,* ashore in 1903 and the *Prevezda* in 1920 and, most recent of all, the large French wooden schooner *Madeleine Tristran* which, if I remember correctly, had a cargo of gin. As a schoolboy, I remember the awesome sound of the thumping as her hull was driven deeper and deeper into the pebbles by the relentless waves. Several years later the wreck was offered to the islanders who brought their axes and chopped her up for firewood.

In 1978 the inn's walls of stone were tested when a great storm swept the seas over the beach demolishing many of the properties in the Square. The *Cove* is a real English pub. No background music, but the character and history encompasses the visitor when he enters.

It has very personal memories for me. I came here to watch a very youthful Hughie Green and the veteran comedian Harry Tate filming *Midshipman Easy* in the 1930s, and in the *Cove Inn,* as a cub newspaperman, I sat and wrote my first 'scoop'. Searching for news, I discovered that a major row was brewing because the owner of the island's Aquarium had decided to call it the Weymouth Aquarium because, he said, Portland was only a sightseeing place for the visitors to the Royal seaside resort.

A Devenish house.

THE CROWN
Fontmell Magna

Fontmell Magna is on the A350 between
Blandford and Shaftesbury.

SHAFTESBURY bound tourists usually stop at Fontmell Magna because they believe that a village with such a lovely name must be beautiful. They are justly rewarded. This village of cottages, by a gentle stream and a dominating 15th century church, is one of the county's showpieces.

They walk around the village and, by the little green, see the site of the old Gossip tree where for 250 years the villagers met and chatted. Dutch Elm disease claimed the old tree in 1976 and it was chopped down with much ceremony and replaced with a sapling. It was said that anyone taking part in the tree's destruction would have bad luck, and for one villager it was true. Shortly after the ceremony 70 year old Frank Hawkins, a bellringer, tugged the church tenor bell and it shattered above his head.

When the visitors have enjoyed the delights of the village, they come to the *Crown Inn* to refresh themselves. A pleasant inn where the hosts serve a good variety of pub grub which you can enjoy against the sound of background music.

The Crown has been in existence since 1890 and once had its own brewery behind it, which is now a Pottery. A beer garden surrounds the car park, with views of the heights of Charlton Down and Zig-Zag Hill, 700 feet above sea level.

A Hall & Woodhouse house.

THE CROWN

Puncknowle

Off the B3157 coast road between Abbotsbury and West Bay. Turn inland at Swyre.

THIS peaceful inn, literally nestling in the shadows of the 12th century church which is caressed by yews and chestnut trees, has surprising and varied historical connections. *The Crown,* 15th century and probably earlier, was originally built as a home for monks. In the 18th century, the inn was the haunt of smugglers led by the infamous Bournemouth based smuggler, Isaac Gulliver, when he opened his western connection. Puncknowle is on the route from Chesil Beach to wealthy customers in Bath. It is said that on one occasion ladies in the bar concealed brandy barrels beneath their flowing skirts, chatting up the Revenue men as they did so. It is also possible that Col. Shrapnel, who invented the terrifying weapon named after him, used the inn as he was a prominent villager.

More recently, it was chosen as the quiet rendezvous of the Portland spies, Ethel Gee and Harry Horton, who plotted around the large open fireplace where logs blaze in winter.

The *Crown Inn,* which has a restaurant and offers accommodation to the travellers enjoying this beautiful and romantic corner of Dorset, sells beer brewed in the town of Bridport. It was in 1794 that beer was first brewed in England's only thatched brewery, a former mill at the junction of the rivers Brit and Asker. The Palmers bought it in the 1800s and the great-grandsons, John and Cleeves Palmer, now run it. They are considering returning to the old system of delivering locally with horse-drawn drays. Visitors are welcome to this unique brewery, which still bears a water wheel.

A Palmers house.

35

THE DRAX ARMS

Bere Regis

*Situated on the main A35 road from Poole to
Dorchester in the heart of the village of
Bere Regis.*

THE early 17th century coaching inn at Bere Regis was called the *King's Head* but 40 years after the land-owning Drax family replaced the Turbervilles in 1733 it became the *Drax Arms* and today has the Drax coat of arms as a colourful inn sign. The first landlord of the *Drax* was called Kitcatt. The toll gate was nearby and there is still stabling at the inn.

The present hosts are keen to restore the pub to its original style. The bar is large, yet friendly and cosy, and the walls are decorated with harness and horse brasses. They have with care opened up the old open fireplace and discovered the original brickwork and quaint salt holes. Signs of the damage caused by the great fire in June 1788, when the inn wore thatch were also discovered. That fire destroyed most of the village and produced a ghost for the *Drax Arms*. She is female and often seen, and makes her presence felt in the bar and kitchen.

The Turberville family who came over with the Conqueror spread their family over the south western counties but this 'right ancient and genteel' family had their main home in Bere Regis, and their canopied tombs are in the church for the visitor to see, as Thomas Hardy did when he used the family as the basis for the D'Urbervilles, and presented them to the world in his famous novel, *Tess of the D'Urbervilles*.

A Hall & Woodhouse inn.

THE DRAX ARMS

Spetisbury

Spetisbury is on the main A350 road from Poole to Blandford.

MANY visitors come to the *Drax Arms* at Spetisbury just to meet a dog called Montgomery. This Staffordshire Bull Terrier boasts the name of Saxon Moor Wingreen Rock, which is rather a mouthful, so the jovial landlord changed the name to Montgomery because he is always on parade and enjoys stepping outside to pose for photographers.

Against a background of soft music, bar food is served until closing time. There is also a beer garden with views of the Stour Valley.

The coat of arms on the inn is a bit of a mystery. Landlord O'Connor has been told that the *Drax* at Spetisbury and the inn of the same name at Bere Regis marked the extremities of the Drax Estate, but the Estate office do not think this is so. They told me that if I looked closely at the coats of arms outside the inns, it will be seen that they are slightly different. They suggest the *Spetisbury Inn* may be named after another branch of the family.

Back to the brewery, Hall and Woodhouse, where they tell me that both houses were purchased from the Drax Estate between 1919 and 1921. The *Drax* at Spetisbury had a thatched roof until fire destroyed it in 1926 and it was rebuilt in the present more modern style.

I can only suggest that the sign painter had a drop too much when painting one of the signs.

A Hall & Woodhouse inn.

DROVERS INN
Gussage All Saints

Off the B3078 main road from Wimborne to Cranborne.

IF you have not ventured Cranborne way over the last few years, you may not have heard of *The Drovers* – a very pleasant old-world inn at Gussage All Saints, the largest of the three Gussage villages near Wimborne St. Giles. It was known for many years as the *Earl Haig* and visitors from the large coastal towns came there to sample the charm of a Dorset inn. It will be remembered because the bar serving area was framed with an enormous gilt frame, which made literally, a living oil painting.

The name was changed because it was thought the famous First World War leader had been commemorated for long enough, and a simple country sounding name would be more appropriate to attract today's customers.

It has lost none of its old charm, and gained by establishing itself as a popular out of town eating place. Speciality is Allen Trout from Lord Shaftesbury's estate fish farm, reared in the little river Allen which flows on to Wimborne to link up with the Stour.

The rejuvenated inn has an elevated lawn with a view of the valley, and a children's play garden. If you come via Wimborne, turn off left at the Knowlton Church turning. That eerie ruin standing in an earthwork is worth a visit.

A free house.

THE FLEUR DE LYS

Cranborne

Cranborne is reached by the B3078 from Wimborne and Bournemouth. The inn is in the centre of the village.

> Oh, we have wandered far and far,
>   We are fordone and wearied quite.
> No lamp is lit: there is no star.
>   Only we know that in the night
> We somewhere missed the faces bright,
>   The lips and eyes we longed to see,
> And Love, and Laughter, and Delight.
>   These things are at the Fleur-de-Lys.

SO wrote Rupert Brook when he stayed at the *Fleur De Lys* in Cranborne, and he was not the only poet to stay at this lovely old inn. Thomas Hardy was a guest when he was writing *Tess,* and a building in the yard – now a garage – was the barn where Tess came to dance in the novel. The infamous Judge Jeffreys also stayed there, but they do not talk about that.

The very noticeable old-world charm of the *Fleur De Lys* is rooted in its ancient origins. Built in the 11th century, alterations over the years have revealed evidence of its original construction. A Gothic arch was discovered on the north side of the building, and two stone pillars on either side of the gateway on the south side of the inn are thought to be ruins from an old monastery in the village. Development of Gothic architecture in France in 1150 may have inspired the choice of a French name for the inn. Renovations to the old lounge fireplace produced evidence and letters proving the building was an inn in the 1600s.

Today the inn is hosted by a young couple who care, and they have kept the village pub atmosphere in an inn which also serves excellent homemade food. They serve tempting soups and steak pies made from ancient local recipes. Charles and Ann Hancock came from the *Blackmore Vale Inn* at Marnhull in the late 1970s and they love the Dorset folklore. Anne makes the rolls and garlic bread and Charles bottles the delicious pickled onions, using a recipe handed down in the village. He is also proud of his wine cellar and makes a speciality of ciders.

One nice touch . . . there is no public bar, but a village bar is an innovation . . . small and cosy and the locals will always welcome you and find time for a chat.

A Hall & Woodhouse house.

FIDDLEFORD INN

Fiddleford

Fiddleford is on the A357 road, just south of Sturminster Newton.

THOSE who love the river Stour come to Fiddleford, just downstream from Sturminster Newton, to see the mill and the spectacular mediaeval Manor House built about 1380. The two storeyed solar wing and half the hall to the east of it remain. One of the features of this fine building is the plaster ceiling of Tudor style. The mill house stands alone reflecting itself in the mill pond which fills from the Stour. This is one of the most peaceful corners of Dorset and you can read the strange inscription carved into the mill wall in 1566. It is an exhortation to the miller written in old English.

The mill was once the hiding place for contraband liquor and it is said that factory workers from Sturminster Newton used to steal from the stores and get themselves fighting drunk.

The nearby 19th century *Fiddleford Inn* was once a brewery and the Adams brothers were brewers and landlords. The old malthouse is now comfortable accommodation, and the archway over the former door covers a smaller entrance today. This free house has previously been called *Travellers Rest* and *Archway House*.

The Wilson family are the hosts at this peaceful inn and serve homemade food.

They have occasional music on Sundays.

A free house.

THE FOX

Ansty

Go north off the A354 at Milborne St.
Andrew. From Milton Abbey follow the road
to Ansty.

A visit to Ansty, as near the heart of Dorset as it is possible to get, is an experience. The village grew up around a brewery and many of the buildings still exist. Today, for instance, the malting house is the village hall. The *Fox Inn* was formerly the grand residence of the brewing Woodhouse family, called Broadclose. Now the flint and brick building is a maze of nooks and crannies to delight drinking folk; a social centre to which visitors flock from all corners of Dorset and further afield.

Charles Hall started to brew beer at Ansty in 1777 and the Woodhouse family became linked with the Halls by marriage, but there has not been a Hall in the business for over 100 years.

The *Fox* is now a free house, and the unique Toby Bar has one of the country's largest displays of the amusing mugs – almost 800 of them. The Platter Bar has a fascinating display of plates and there are fine prints on the walls throughout the house. People come from far afield to sample the food at the Fox, and Egon Ronay chose it as his first Pub of the Year in 1980.

The Village Bar, favoured by locals in summer, is a farm wagon transformed into a serving bar. The Children's Room contains a large variety of games and the skittle alley, with its own bar, can be used as a private functions room.

One word of warning to the newcomer. Do not sit in Alfred's Chair in the corner of the Toby Bar. It is the property of 74 year old Alf Humber, the last maltster in the old brewery. It is marked with a plate.

A free house.

THE FOX INN

Corfe Castle

The Fox is situated just off the Square in the shadow of the Church and Town Hall.

HUMBLE it may look from outside, but the *Fox* at Corfe Castle has always been my favourite Dorset inn. For many long years its landlord, Teddy Brown, was not only a character at his own inn but was known throughout the county. Short and rotund, this jovial man of Poole would entertain with Dorset yarns for hours on end if he liked you and, if he did not, he was just as likely to send you around the corner to another hostelry.

The inn was a residence 100 years before the great castle was blown up in 1645, and changed its construction very little when it became an inn. From the street you enter directly into the bar with wooden benches, and a serving hatch through the 18 inch thick walls. Another hatch off this central barrel room provides service to customers in the passageway, and a cosy lounge is situated beyond this.

Teddy Brown always had something under the counter to show his friends – a bottle of vintage cider or, as he would boast, some secretly made Blue Vinny cheese, or even a rare document or relic of Corfe. The inn was the clearing house for such things, and regulars brought them in so that Teddy would display them in the Corfe Museum opposite, which he 'kept an eye on.' 'I keeps the lights on late so that people are drawn to the inn', he quipped, and when the church and Castle were floodlit, he would cunningly turn one of the lights so that the *Fox* received some illumination.

I would never pass through Corfe without calling on my old friend and, now that he has gone, his daughter and grandson run the inn and keep alive the friendly atmosphere, and you will meet jovial regulars who have used the *Fox* for decades.

Visitors who call on Shrove Tuesday can observe the ancient customs of the Purbeck Marblers and Stonemasons. To be initiated, new apprentices have to carry a loaf and a quart of ale from the *Fox* into the Town Hall opposite, where the meeting is held. They have to run a gauntlet of thirsty quarrymen who constantly relieve the lads of their ale.

Many famous people have been made honorary members of the quaint order including Elisabeth Muntz, the sculptress, and a former Bishop of Salisbury who was loth to be photographed with ale in his hand. 'I shall be getting letters for weeks', he said as he downed a pint of bitter. Other strange events include the kicking of a football through the streets and the handing over of a pound of pepper as rent.

The beer garden is a retreat in summer. Quaint, like the inn itself, the little lawn is beyond the kitchen garden. Visitors sit on a rough rustic seat shaded by a veteran apple tree, and listen in peace to the insects and songbirds. But towering above is the Castle ruin to remind of the village's cruel and bloody past.

A Whitbread house.

THE GLOBE

Herston

Situated on the Herston roundabout as you enter Swanage from Wareham.

THE *Globe* at Herston is an old coaching inn near the roundabout as you enter Swanage. A quiet house which former Swanage fireman Michael Bower runs with his wife Margaret, following his father and grandfather before him. The family have run the 300 year old inn since soon after the turn of the century.

Like so many Dorset inns, it has a Cromwell connection – but this one is rather macabre. It is said that the cellar was used as a mortuary in those troubled days. When horse-propelled traffic was at its peak, the three stables at the inn catered for the horse and cart trade, providing a repair depot for the vehicles.

Regulars play the strange game of shove a halfpenny on the long board – a sport peculiar to the Purbecks, and have a successful quiz team.

There is a beer garden and children are welcome. Simple bar catering is based around ploughmans lunches and cheese.

Gentle background music does not destroy the friendly conversation in this inn of little bars, but may be shouted down by Polly – the parrot who has been in residence for forty years.

A Whitbread house.

GAGGLE OF GEESE

Buckland Newton

Beyond the Piddle valley out of Dorchester or Puddletown. The village is off the B3143 road.

BUCKLAND Newton, beneath softly rounded hills at the head of the Blackmore Vale, was in 1937 named by the BBC as the typical Dorset village, but it is so tucked away just off the B3143 highway that I only seem to find it when I am lost.

The only surviving inn at this peaceful village, which once boasted a cheese factory and a sawmill, is the *Gaggle of Geese* – a free house formerly known as the *Royal Oak*. In spite of extensive alterations during the middle 1970s, which included the uncovering of an ancient fireplace and the building of a skittle alley and games room, it is the very warm and friendly personalities of the joint landlords, Peter Jones and Sue Cook, that draw you to this hostelry. An excellent inn sign depicting flying geese painted by a local artist, Len Prylle, hangs near the pond where the resident geese play.

The 150 year old inn was formerly a shop and occasionally local musicians entertain in the bar.

In the nearby 13th century church there is a tablet in memory of Thomas Barnes who died eight years after Shakespeare. He was the wealthy ancestor of the Rev. William Barnes, Dorset dialect poet, the centenary of whose death was celebrated in 1986.

Buckland Newton is best approached from Puddletown via the Piddle valley.

A free house.

GEORGE INN
Reforne – Portland

*Turn right when you approach Easton
Square, along Reforne Street for half a mile,
until a lonely church comes into view. The
George is on the left.*

THE *George Inn* stands on one of the bleakest and topmost heights of the island of Portland – that bleak mass of stone which has provided material for many famous buildings. The village of Reforne is near the cliffs which face the full force of gales sweeping up the Channel. On a stormy night you will hear the thud of waves breaking on the Tar rocks in Clay Hope Cove, and this coast along the West Weare has claimed many ships. It was not a stormy night when I made my first visit to *The George* in 1936, but a calm foggy Sunday evening when the 20,000 ton liner *Winchester Castle* just glided onto the rocks beneath nearby Blacknor Fort. As the fog lifted, it appeared from the clifftop that a mighty hotel ablaze with lights had sprung up at the cliff base.

Not far from Easton Square the inn, whose thick walls offer protection from the wind, has stood since Jacobean times. It is the oldest dwelling house on the island built, of course, from Portland stone. The entrance is the traditional low stone porch, well-known at Portland. It was originally the Clerk's House where the court leets were held and a rare reeve staff, over 100 years old, hangs in the low ceilinged, cosy bar.

Do not be fooled by the humble exterior of this ancient inn with its crude sign, because as well as the cosy bar with log fire, there is a 50 seater restaurant serving excellent food.

The colourful inn sign stands out amongst the dull grey buildings. It depicts the king.

A Devenish house.

THE HALF MOON

Sherborne

*Sherborne is 40 miles up the Stour valley
from Bournemouth via A350 and A357, and
A3030 from Sturminster Newton, or the
A352 from Dorchester.*

SHERBORNE, one of Dorset's loveliest towns, is a place of much dignity and dominated by the ancient abbey and public school. At the heart of the shopping centre in Half Moon Street is the *Half Moon Hotel*. This old coaching inn literally had a face lift in 1936, when the front wall was demolished and rebuilt with the same bricks 15 feet back, to give a forecourt.

It is well executed and complements the older part of the building. In the coach entrance, the old pump for providing water for the horses still stands, but thoughtless hands demolished the old wooden trough into which it fed.

Before the Second World War the great dining hall was always filled with farming folk on market days, the sun streaming through the windows onto the whiter than white aprons and caps of the waitresses, and on the great show of silver at the far end of the room. Today it has kept its country image but with sophisticated decor, more in keeping with the 1980s. But the sun still shines into the dining room and tastefully decorated carvery of this Toby house.

In 1943 a stray enemy bomb almost hit the inn but landed in gardens behind.

Sherborne was the scene of the Bryant murder case in 1936, and eventually Mrs. Charlotte Bryant was one of the last women hanged in the county. The investigation shook the placid calm of the abbey town and the Scotland Yard detectives who, in those days, were distinguished by the wearing of bowler hats, became well-known as they prepared their case against a woman who poisoned her husband. When it was all over, the Scotland Yard men Chief Inspector Alec Bell and Det. Sgt. Topsell, Dorset police officials and Press bade farewell to each other at a get-together held in the tap room of the *Plume of Feathers,* an ancient inn now no longer serving the public but still retaining its right to re-open. It was an unusual get-together around the barrels standing in the centre of the stone flagged tap room, opposite the abbey. Press and police who had been following their own leads and thoughts for several weeks chatted freely about the murder. The Scotland Yard men even took off their bowlers.

A Toby house.

HALF
MOON
INN
Melplash

Melplash is off the A3066 road between
Bridport and Beaminster.

A spectral figure garbed in a dark grey coachman's long half-coped cloak, and wearing a white scarf, is a resident ghost at the *Half Moon Inn* at Melplash – a village north of Bridport. After listening to the host's stories of this 40–50 year old figure's frequent appearances in the bar, I found myself holding tightly to my ale, lest the ghost be a thirsty one.

A more concrete feature of this 300 year old inn, which stands in line with the old schoolhouse and the church, is a 40 foot-deep open well behind the bar. The host does not appreciate jokes about its presence being connected with watering the beer. This is a 'locals' pub of great character serving bar snacks from sandwiches to steaks. Children are welcome and there is a peaceful beer garden.

If the ghost of the *Half Moon* is an odd character, he follows in the footsteps of a real life strange resident of a long time ago. In the reign of Henry VIII the Sheriff of Dorset was a Sir Thomas More, a jovial hard-drinking character. One night after a heavy session of imbibing, he rode into Dorchester and ordered the release of all the prisoners in the gaol. The reluctant warders opened the gates and as the highwaymen, pickpockets and sheepstealers rushed down the main street and scattered into open country, Sir Thomas cheered them on.

Next morning, as you can imagine, he found himself in serious trouble. He got out of it, but that is another amusing story.

A Palmers house.

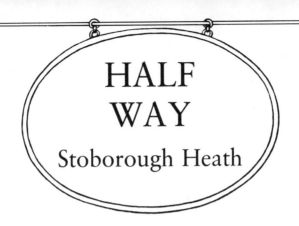

HALF WAY

Stoborough Heath

Midway along the main Wareham to Corfe road – A351

THE road across Stoborough Heath from Wareham to Corfe has been the scene of horrendous historical events. King Edward galloped along it with a dagger in his back, murdered by his stepmother, Queen Elfrida, at Corfe in AD 978. Later, Peter of Pomfret was dragged behind a horse and hanged at Wareham by the order of King John.

Midway along this road today is a typical Dorset inn. White walled and tidily thatched, the Half Way has cosy little bars in a building that was probably once a farm house which brewed its own beer.

The charm of this quiet inn drawing the trade of passing tourists is probably the fact that the landlady has lived there for 50 years. She came as a small child and, much later, took over the tenancy from her mother and father. Formerly a Strongs house, it now carries the banner of Whitbread.

She welcomes you to her home and offers pub meals in peaceful surroundings. There is no music and, on a sunny day, outside tables offer a view of the heath.

Regulars have formed a quiz team, which does well in local events, and the inn is proud of its darts performers.

A Whitbread house.

THE HAMBRO ARMS
Milton Abbas

*Milton Abbas, near famous Bulbarrow Hill,
is reached by turning north off the A354
midway between Dorchester and Blandford.*

VISITORS come to Milton Abbas to see the 18th century village built by Squire Damer, who razed a whole town to the ground because it stood around the Minster and where he wanted to build his mansion. He lawned the site of the town and rebuilt a village out of his sight just over the hill to house the townsfolk. A village of 40 identical cottages was built like dolls' houses evenly spaced each side of a main wide road cut into a fold on the North Dorset chalk hills.

The Milton Abbas he destroyed had a fine brewery. This was not rebuilt, but in the new complex you will find the *Hambro Arms,* an inn of great charm, half-way up the hillside of this single street village.

The inn offers the traveller a restaurant service of good food with morning and evening meals. From the front of this picturesque pub you look down the cottaged street with wide lawns separating thatched homes from the road. Once there were chestnut trees between each of the cottages but, diseased, they were cut down several years ago.

On your way from unique Milton Abbas village to visit the Abbey, you pass a peaceful picture book lake nestling at the foot of a forested hillside.

A Devenish house.

THE HAVEN

Mudeford

On the Mudeford Spit via Stanpit Road out of Christchurch.

THE *Haven House Inn* stands on Mudeford Spit at the mouth of Christchurch Harbour – a lovely little hamlet abused by the fact that most of it has now been given over to car parks. The inn, in spite of some modernisation, has retained much of the old charm nestling beside the picturesque Dutch style cottages, but the fishing nets and stained photographs which once adorned the walls have gone from this famous fishermen's inn.

The *Haven House* is nearly 300 years old and was at the centre of the Bloody Battle of Mudeford in July 1784, in which the sloop of war, *Orestes*, opened fire on smugglers ferrying casks of brandy ashore near the inn. It would seem that half the population of Christchurch and Stanpit were getting the contraband off the beach and hiding it. The *Orestes'* Sailing Master led a party ashore demanding the smugglers surrendered, but they opened fire from the dunes and killed him. It was a victory for the 'Gentlemen of the Night' and chain shot from the *Orestes*, which hit the roof of the inn, was preserved and is now in Christchurch museum.

This picturesque inn is still the meeting place for the local fishermen who will book you in for a fishing trip as you down your pint and, of course, the sea food is prominent on the menu.

Picnic tables encourage many visitors outdoors to drink and enjoy the ozone at the same time.

A Devenish house.

HORSE
& GROOM
Wareham

In the Market Square near Wareham Quay.

WAREHAM, on a crossroads where visitors take the routes to reach their favourite watering places on the Dorset coast, is ignored by most in the rush to get to the sea, and more so now that a bypass sweeps the westbound traffic clear of this ancient walled town. Yet Wareham is steeped in history and was one of the earliest human settlements in the county. Once it was a leading seaport, and the town provided three ships and 59 men for Edward III's fleet when he prepared for the siege of Calais in 1347.

This typical old English inn has retained its character and is a social centre for residents and visitors. The hosts hold pensioners evenings with sandwiches supplied, and singalongs around the piano are popular. Most mornings you will find some of the town's old worthies gathering in the bar, and some will spin a lively yarn often in dialect.

Older Dorset imbibers will remember the now closed Lord Nelson at the foot of the wall near the Church of St. Martin. A one time landlord, who had a false leg, would challenge new-comers to a game of darts. He usually lost and, in great anger, would plunge darts into his knee – to the dismay of his opponents. Then, to the amusement of regulars, he would remove the darts, lift his trousers and display the wooden joint. He did the act so often that the joint looked as if it had a bad case of woodworm.

A Whitbread house.

THE HORNS INN

Colehill

Colehill is a mile out of Wimborne. Turn right off the B3078 Cranborne bound road.

READERS in their middle seventies will remember the original *Horns Inn* at Colehill near Wimborne – a low cottage style building cosied in thick Dorset thatch. A fire in 1929 ended its days and the Wimborne brewers, Ellis, built the brick house we know today. It is rumoured that they built it as a residence, but it was as a pub that they sold it to Hall and Woodhouse in the early 1930s. It stands alone on a country crossroads and visitors sit on an elevated terrace and enjoy Dorset countryside framed in magnificent bushes. In the summer, the inn is known for its bountiful flower baskets hanging from the eaves.

Ivor and Rosemary Thomas are the hosts at this popular inn where homemade specials are served at the bar morning and evening.

The collection of 400 tankards, jugs and chamber pots hanging from the beams are worth seeing.

Ivor hails from London but has a country connection. His father ran a herd of cows in Stepney – one of the last in central London.

The inn has soothing background music.

A Hall & Woodhouse inn.

THE ILCHESTER ARMS
Abbotsbury

Abbotsbury is on the B3157 road from Weymouth.

D O not be put off by the outward appearance of the *Ilchester Arms* at Abbotsbury, with its strange porched entrance off centre from the main part of a symmetrical building, because inside there is the warmth and happy atmosphere of a Dickensian coaching inn.

The house belongs to the Ilchester Estate and specialises in English home cooked food. Once you are inside the inn, leaving the dour main street of the village behind, you are in for another surprise – because you get a view of a peaceful garden and patio with a whispering fountain and, in the background, the hilltop chapel of St. Catherine, landmark to generations of seafaring men coming up Channel, and a watch house and signal station for the 'Gentlemen of the Night'.

Before you come to the *Ilchester Arms,* browse around this lovely village – very Cotswold in style. You will sense its ancient history. There was an Abbey here 500 years ago and the church still bears holes from the shots fired in the Civil Wars. The great barn, 276 feet long, still stands almost intact like a fine cathedral next to a lily-clad pond where the monks once caught their fish. That is when they were not dining on swan. The famous swannery was created for the purpose of feeding the monks.

The *Ilchester Arms* has no music and children are welcome in the dining rooms.

In the smuggling days it was the headquarters for infamous smuggler, Isaac Gulliver, but at that time it was known as the *Ship Inn.*

A Devenish house.

THE ILCHESTER ARMS

Symondsbury

Symondsbury is on a right hand loop off the A35, two miles out of Bridport going west.

FEW will deny that the most beautiful part of Dorset is in the wild western area, where fields spread in valleys and on hillsides like an enormous patchwork blanket roughly thrown down. It is in the folds of this blanket that some of Dorset's loveliest villages can be found, almost hidden from the fast highways of modern living.

Such a village is Symondsbury which is on a country lane off the A35 just west of Bridport.

Here is a picture postcard village, church, school and inn all clustered in a valley almost unchanged through centuries. The villagers are proud of their place and, in recent times, became angry over the felling of an 80 foot oak tree. When gamekeeper Jack Cook died in the 1970s, he left his cider press to the villagers who still annually make their own brew.

The *Ilchester Arms* is in keeping with the atmosphere of this friendly village, and young hosts make the stranger feel at home. 'We are part of the spontaneous village life', they say. 'We have a skittle alley and enjoy folk singing'. They serve homemade food at lunchtime and evening.

A strange thing about this truly rural place – it had its own electric light supply nearly a decade before the town of Bridport.

Major Sir Philip Colfox formed the Symondsbury Electric Light Co., and the local blacksmith made the lamp standards.

A Devenish house.

THE JOLLY SAILOR

Poole

*This inn stands on Poole Quay and is known
to mariners the world over.*

I find it amusing that the *Jolly Sailor* and the *Lord Nelson* stand next to each other, separated only by the former Blue Boar Lane, because the famous Admiral is seldom portrayed as a laughing boy. The *Jolly Sailor* has its roots back in the late 18th century and, for many decades, was a boisterous seaman's pub. Today the inn has a new image and, with its log cabin decor, draws thousands of visitors who come to see this well known hostelry.

The hosts are proud of their traditional beers and spirits drawn from the wood. They serve fish dishes amongst other fare at lunch time. Country and Western duos entertain and, sometimes, a Barber Shop quartet.

For almost 70 years, from 1907, the *Jolly Sailor* had the Davis family as landlords. The famous Harry Davis dived into the harbour on numerous occasions to rescue drowning people. It has been said that sometimes revellers drew lots after closing time to select one of their number who would jump in the harbour, so that Harry would dash across the quay to effect a rescue. This waggish joke is not true and, on the walls of the inn, were three Royal Humane Society certificates and an Illuminated Address from Poole Council commemorating his service and the fact that he had saved many from drowning.

A Whitbread house.

THE
KING CHARLES
INN
Poole

*Situated in Thames Street, behind the pillared
former Harbour Office.*

CUNNING smugglers and infamous pirates feature in the story
of Poole, the ancient Dorset port and most of the old
harbourside inns have had connections with the 'Gentlemen
of the Night'. In 1364 the Barons of Winchelsea granted Poole a
Charter defining her sea and fishing bounds. Quayside inns play a
role when the Admiral and Mayor of the Port goes afloat with
pomp and ceremony to affirm his rights. For twenty years I was a
Pirate of Poole doing my part in trying to mar the proceedings.
The townsfolk were wary on Bounds beating days when the
pirates landed. A bank manager was once abducted and 'hanged'
and on another occasion there was consternation when town
barmaids were captured and chained to lamp posts in the High
Street.

There are some inns where the feeling of the past is so strong
that it seems wrong to pass through the entrance in modern dress.
Such a place is the *King Charles*. Here the illusion is intensified
because it is part of Poole Quay which looks like a permanent film
set. The Georgian Custom House, the Stone Town Cellars and the
old pillared Harbour Office combine with the inn to make a
memorial backcloth to Poole's great days as a port.

The enthusiasm of Brian Elderfield, Mine Host of the *King
Charles Inn,* has provided the town with what is probably Dorset's
most unique hostelry. The inn, circa 1550, was originally known
as the *New Inn,* but renamed after King Charles of France landed
at Poole Quay having fled his native country aboard the English
Package Ship *Great Britain*. The original small bars have been

opened up to expose 16th century panelling which, like the rest of the inn, is protected as an historic building.

Brian Elderfield is a keen member of the Society of Poole Men, who fight enthusiastically to preserve old Poole. He finds himself in a dilemma when the sea bounds of the port are beaten because, as a member of the Admiral's jury, he has to tolerate the colourful pirates who invade his bar.

His alterations include the incorporation of the ancient Kynges Halle next door and restoration to its 15th century style. A fine vaulted roof and an open fireplace are featured. The former's beams, 600 years old, are thought to be the frames of a ship inverted. This building was once part of the Town Cellars before Thames Street was cut through, and was, at one time, thought to

be the longest building in England. It has had many uses – Custom Store, Wool House and, more recently, the base for the Johnny Onions salesmen from Brittany.

Sea food is featured on the menu of the *King Charles*, which retains the character of a smugglers' inn, and at weekends solo artistes provide entertainment.

A Whitbread house.

THE KING'S ARMS

Blandford

Situated in White Cliff Mill Street in the centre of the town.

THEY will show you a cosy bar at the *King's Arms Hotel* in Blandford which, in the 18th century, was a tallow maker's premises. On June 4th 1731, a fire started in the room and spread so rapidly that nearly all the town of Blandford was burned down. The firemen watched their engine perish early in the fire and, by eleven at night, gave up their fight to save the church – and that too was razed to the ground. It is known as the Great Fire because conflagration-prone Blandford had also suffered devastating fires in 1579, 1644, 1677 and 1713.

Out of the ashes of the Great Fire, two local architects emerged – the Bastard brothers – who rebuilt the magnificent market town in a tidy Georgian style. Blandford Forum takes its name from being a market place situated on one of the chief fords of the sleepy Stour, Dorset's main river.

It is a pleasant drive to Blandford from the coast, either by the road which leads through Wimborne and the long avenue of trees beyond Kingston Lacey, or via Sturminster Marshall and Spetisbury on the other bank of the Stour.

Adjacent to the hotel is a derelict brewery which once provided the ale.

A Bass house.

THE KINGS ARMS
Portesham

Portesham is on the B3157 out of Weymouth.

A bar fitted out in the colours and style of Captain Masterman Hardy's quarters aboard HMS *Victory* is a novelty in the *Kings Arms* at Portesham, near Abbotsbury. The village is proud of the man in whose arms Nelson died at Trafalgar, and a monument to him stands on a hilltop near the village.

He was a great beer drinker and once proclaimed, 'Beer was the best ever drunk if it comes from Possum.' This being his name for Portesham.

The inn is known to children as the pub with a pink pig up a tree. The tree standing in the centre of a large and peaceful beer garden, where youngsters can play with the goats.

The *Kings Arms* is a good old fashioned Dorset inn which holds singsongs around the piano, and background tapes sometimes project 'oldies' such as George Formby.

I like the motto in the bar, 'It's nice to be important, but important to be nice.'

Some years before the last war, I was party to a wicked silly season newspaper hoax at this inn. With some colleagues, we were drinking in a pub at Morton bemoaning the fact that there was so little news about. Someone said 'Let's file a story about cat racing, using an electric mouse.' The ale had been flowing freely and ringing the landlord of the *Kings Arms,* we told him of our plot and that we had decided his inn should be the venue. If any London newspaper rang him to check the story he was to tell them that it had taken place but it had now stopped. The story misfired. It was the era when wire machines for transmitting photographs

76

had made their appearance, and we were confronted with the news that one national daily had already sent a wire man and would we stage a picture. We all dashed to Portesham, rounded up and borrowed a few cats and, holding them on the bar, had one sat on kitchen scales to create a weigh-in picture. It appeared next day and, of course, a row ensued. The local vicar said it was disgraceful as did some of the residents. Others were annoyed because they did not know about it. I think that most people realised it was a hoax and the incident was soon forgotten.

A Devenish house.

LANGTON ARMS

Tarrant Monkton

Tarrant Monkton can be reached by turning off the Wimborne to Blandford, Badbury Rings road (B3082) at Tarrant Keyneston and following the road along the Tarrant valley for 2 miles.

THE river Tarrant flows through eight miles of beautiful Dorset farmland, giving its name to eight villages along its course. Midway, where a ford crossing gives access to a compact and comely hamlet called Tarrant Monkton, is the *Langton Arms* – a lovely thatched inn nestling in the shadow of the flint and stone built church. Although a long way from the coast, it is a popular eating place specialising in homemade cooking.

At the rear of this inn is a very large room, now well-decorated and used as a private games room for hire. During the First World War it was added as a social centre for men of the Naval Division who trained at Tarrant Hinton, two miles distant. At night they crowded the very long bar, sparse of decoration and stretching the length of the building, and quaffed good English ale . . . the bleak walls echoing their laughter and bawdy stories. The peaceful Tarrant valley was their last memory of the old country, because they went to Gallipoli and nearly all perished in that dreadful holocaust of war. High on a hilltop nearby is an obelisk erected to their memory by the handful who came back.

The lovely valley has much to offer the countryside explorer, and the villagers of Monkton take pride in keeping their place as a showpiece.

A free house.

THE LORD NELSON
Poole

*This inn stands on Pool Quay and is known
to mariners the world over.*

JIM Kellaway, Mine Host of the *Lord Nelson,* is a landlord of
the old school ... a character seeking ideas to promote this
popular inn, and encouraging customers to take an interest in
charity events. The harbour raft race is a popular innovation, as
well as the dawn visit from Morris dancers on May Day. The
customers have supported the Lord Nelson Jubilee Sailing Trust
and their giant square rigger, which gives the disabled equal
opportunities to sail, and have already raised £7000. They run a
sponsored marathon from Hengistbury Head to Poole Quay
annually, and in 1986 the runners were paced by board sailors
who made the trip by sea.

The interior of the pub, which has linked bars, is decorated with
memorabilia of a nautical nature. Photographs depict a wide range
of battleships and yachts, including HMS *Nelson* firing a broad-
side, and yachts of the famous J class fleet. Recent acquisitions to
this nautical museum include relics from the Falklands conflict,
such as a masthead light from HMS *Bulwark,* and a brass gun
base which the landlord – a keen diver – brought up from Poole
Bay.

In 1764 the original *Blue Boar Inn* was built on the site of a turf
house. It became the *Nelson* in 1811 and the *Lord Nelson* in 1818.
Jim runs the inn with his wife, Sheila, and they serve food at the
bar at lunchtime.

Artists Augustus John and Henry Lamb were once customers
and the former was summoned for leaving his car without lights

80

outside the *Lord Nelson*. Somewhere in the building is a message in a bottle placed in a cavity during alterations in the 1920s, by Augustus John. When it was sealed up, he scrawled on the wall in tar: 'We rolled back the stone but the Lord riz not.' The inn has a children's room and an ale garden.

A Hall & Woodhouse house.

THE MANOR HOTEL
West Bexington

West Bexington is reached by turning off the B3157 at Swyre, between Abbotsbury and Bridport.

WEST Bexington is a little hamlet of bungalows on the slopes which reach up from the Chesil Beach between Abbotsbury and Bridport. Its beginnings are centuries old and the Manor House, now the *Manor Hotel,* had star rating in the Domesday Book. But the friendly hosts will tell you with a smile that the comforts and facilities have improved since then. Oak Jacobean panelling above stone-flagged floors greet you on entry and the dining room looks out over a rose garden to the blue waters of West Bay beyond. Descend a stone spiral staircase to the cellar bar and you are in a drinking man's paradise.

In the early 1930s a wealthy developer had the idea of creating a seaside resort to be known as Bexington-on-Sea. He built a swimming pool and I was surprised to see it is still there today. A concrete basin with decades of weeds growing through the cracks because before the developer had completed the pool, he went out of business.

So the hamlet was spared for those who care for a peaceful place by the sea, and are prepared to descend the narrow lane which leads down from the B3157 road.

The menu features duck and fish, and the hotel holds special evenings such as Burns Night when haggis is served, and there is Scotch beef on Edwardian occasions. The tea room is cosy with chintz curtains framing the windows. The host is proud of his range of real ales.

The Manor House was used by generations of the Napier family who although living at nearby Puncknowle, used Bexington as a summer residence, and by younger members as a home in time of trouble. The Napiers, sometimes called Napper, descended from merchants who sold fish to the Abbey at Abbotsbury.

Robert Napier who was knighted in 1681 was probably responsible for rebuilding Bexington in the latter half of the 17th century and lived at the Manor House, now the hotel.

An earlier Napier, who joined the Middle Temple in 1586, was member for Dorchester in the 1590s and on his death left an almshouse for ten poor men in Dorchester. The building still exists in South street and called Nappers Mite.

A free house.

THE MARTYRS INN
Tolpuddle

Tolpuddle is on the main A35 road between Dorchester and Poole, about 6 miles from Dorchester.

ALTHOUGH *The Martyrs Inn* at Tolpuddle is a fairly modern building, it does not forget that the village is chained to history by the exploits of the 'Six Men of Dorset' who protested that their wages as agricultural workers were too small, and were sent to a penal colony for their trouble. So after the visitor has looked around this little village, with a main street lined by snug thatched cottages, and has spent a while beneath the rotting Martyrs' Tree where the six met to discuss their problems in the early 1800s . . . he or she can adjourn to *The Martyrs Inn*. A special Martyrs Bar has the warm brick walls decorated with old prints and harness once used by horses working in the fields around.

The *Martyrs,* although tastefully conveying a country village style, was built in 1929 and originally called *The Crown.* A wise public relations man renamed the inn in 1979. Bar food is served.

The original premises built in the 1850s, where home brewed beer was sold, were pulled down to make way for the fast Poole to Dorchester road which now runs over the site.

The *Martyrs* does not entertain performing musical groups, and the six martyrs would probably be pleased about that as they were devout Methodists.

It would have been worthwhile if the authorities had bypassed the heart of the village, which is a tourist attraction for visitors from all over the world, because on the little triangle of green beside the Martyrs Tree, there is a peace and tranquillity which makes you aware that you are standing where history was made.

Near the inn is a small museum which tells the story of the rural trade unionists. It is surrounded by six memorial cottages.

A Hall & Woodhouse house.

THE NEW INN
Wareham

On the banks of the Frome at Wareham Quay.

IT is difficult to understand why Wareham's lovely and historic quay is given over for use as a car park, when there is so much land around the little town, but behind the regimented cars is the ancient *New Inn* – about 250 years old.

A pleasant evening run from Weymouth, Bournemouth, Poole, Swanage or Christchurch brings you to this place on the banks of the river Frome, to which yachts come through the reeds of Poole harbour by the same route as the pillaging Danes and the trading craft of the Romans, centuries ago.

For many years it was the headquarters of the Muddlecombe Gang who attended carnivals all over the south of England. The then landlord was chief of the gang of comedians who included amongst their number a blacksmith, a 'pot' boy at a local hotel who was a brilliant cornet player, a clown, an attendant at a sewage farm and a press photographer (myself). They claimed to have used the name Muddlecombe before the famous comedian, Rob Wilton, and entertained at events, on and off their float. Carnival goers will remember such sketches as the Muddlecombe Fire Brigade, the Boy Scouts, the Laundry and the Grannydears Band, performed at leading towns.

Hot and cold snacks are served from the bar.

A Whitbread house.

NEW LONDON TAVERN

Poole

The New London Tavern is in Lagland
Street in Old Poole, near the Town Quay.

THE New London Tavern is a building of Old Poole that has survived the bulldozer and has been renovated in keeping with the more elegant buildings which now line Lagland Street. It is very much a locals' pub, only 100 years old, but I include it in this book because of an amusing story concerning my past. It is where I sat and sulked after being 'drummed out of the Brownies.' In nearby Skinner Street there used to be a meeting hall, and it was here that Lady Baden Powell was addressing a gathering of Brownies, who listened spellbound to their leader. I was assigned to record the event way back in the 1950s, and Lady Baden Powell took strong exception to my flashbulbs and ordered me out. Feeling a bit silly at such a public rebuke in front of children, I stormed into the New London Tavern and ordered a pint.

Realising that I was deeply offended, her Ladyship sent a senior Guiding Officer to find me and apologise. I cannot think how this lady knew where to kind me, but she did and I mellowed in the spell of her charm. The story got back to Fleet Street and I became known as the only British press photographer not only to be drummed out of the Brownies, but by none other than the Queen Bee herself.

An Eldridge Pope house.

THE
RED LION
Sturminster Newton

The inn is reached by taking the A350 from Blandford and transferring to the A357 at Durweston.

THE *Red Lion* at Sturminster Newton stands amongst cottages of thatch on the hill above the river Stour on the Sherborne road. Until 1952 the gypsies, with their colourful horse-drawn wagons, pulled in to have their wagon wheels bonded at the blacksmith's forge behind the inn. Amongst the personalities who had their horses shod was dialect broadcaster, author and farmer, Ralph Wightman. The last blacksmith was Percy Stockley, a traditional smith, burly, clean-shaven with well muscled arms. I remember him because once, at the end of an interview, he led me into the Snug bar of the *Red Lion* and, without asking my preference, ordered me 'a pint of the best in the house' and, from the tone of his voice, the landlord would not have served anything but the best.

The Forge has long been destroyed and the Snug bar is incorporated into the large 'Potty' bar with a unique open fireplace in the centre of the room using the old Snug chimney, and burning sweet-smelling logs.

The hosts at this Hall and Woodhouse inn serve bar food each lunchtime, and evenings also on Friday and Sunday. The host is a motor car fanatic and the walls of the inn are adorned with interesting photographs and posters from the car racing world.

William Barnes, the Dorset dialect poet, used to pass the inn on his way to school in the early 1800s, but I doubt if the old parson ever went inside.

A Hall & Woodhouse inn.

ROSE AND CROWN

Birdsmoorgate

Situated on a lonely crossroads where the B3165 from Lyme to Crewkerne crosses the Chard to Bridport road.

THE *Rose & Crown* is one of the highest inns in the county and is to Dorset what Ted Moult's Pennines inn, featured in television advertisements, is to the northerners. Its lights at night can be seen from hills miles around. In olden days I could imagine a highwayman waiting at this crossroads, which affords a magnificent view of the Marshwood Vale. But brutal murder features in its history, and left behind a door rattling ghost.

Forty-five year old Martha Brown lived opposite the inn in a cottage, in the 1850s, with her husband John – almost half her age. He was a traveller. On his travels he met and had an affair with another younger woman. Jealous Martha found out and murdered him with a hatchet, throwing the remains down a well. The inquest was held at the *Rose & Crown* and after trial Martha was sentenced to be hanged. It was the last public execution at Dorchester and was witnessed by a very young Thomas Hardy, who was so shocked that he mentions it in his *Tess of the d'Urbervilles*.

The inn today is a happy social centre recently refurbished with a cream wash on the exterior. That it is run by a friendly family is very obvious.

A Burtons brewery supplies them with their featured beer, Crown Ale, a real ale which 'reaches the roots'. This accompanies five other bitters, some with strange names like Weedkiller and Old Hookey.

This ancient and cosy inn can trace its deeds and displays them from 1721.

Soft background music adds to the charm of this West Dorset pub, where the memory of Martha Brown lives on through a rattling door.

A free house.

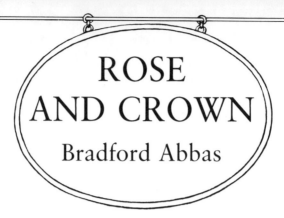

ROSE AND CROWN

Bradford Abbas

*The village of Bradford Abbas nestles along
a peaceful road which loops south of the
main A30 road between Yeovil and
Sherborne, near Dorset's northern boundary
with Somerset, about 40 miles from the
coast. All routes from east and south lead
you through rich and beautiful farming land.*

THERE is no other need to come to Bradford Abbas except to admire its ancient church, and visit the *Rose and Crown* standing beneath the 90 foot mediaeval tower of one of the finest churches in Dorset. With its canopied niches on the west front, it resembles a small cathedral. When the visitor has had enough of this fine building, with 15th century panelled roof and beautiful Jacobean pulpit, and has marvelled at the warmth of the gold Liassic limestone from which the village is shaped, he should ponder in silence, because this place is a thousand years old, and then enter the large rambling bar of the *Rose and Crown*. The building was erected in the 15th century and thought to be a monk's retreat. Bradford Abbas was a satellite of Sherborne and some of the land was given by King Alfred to the Abbots in AD933.

Later the building saw service as a malthouse and, since 1539, it has been the village inn. The long cosy bar has a grand fireplace enhanced with ancient panelling above. Home-made snacks and meals are served seven days a week and the inn has all the requirements of a community centre, including beer garden, skittle alley and games room.

It is not the inn's antiquity which brought it 20th century fame, but the habits of four regulars in the 1930s, whose story the brewers turned to their advantage in an amusing advertising stunt.

Five of the inn's male customers had a total age of 444 years and they were filmed by Movietone News as they quaffed their pints through enormous white beards. It brought them national fame and Sam Ring (92), Thomas Coombs (91), James Higgins (89), George Chaney (89) and Sid Parsons (83) came to town to see themselves on the big screen. But the fact that the village also had five 'old girls', with ages totalling 427 years – one aged 91 – was kept secret at the time. They said they did not want to spoil the glory for the boys, but it was more likely that they did not wish to reveal their ages.

The old newsreel is kept in the village and shown on special occasions.

An Eldridge Pope house.

ROSE AND CROWN
Long Burton

The Rose and Crown is on the A352 between Dorchester and Sherborne, four miles out of Sherborne.

IF you like dogs, you will be at home at the *Rose and Crown,* Long Burton. When the door is opened, a young impetuous Jack Russell named Mackeson, and Shep, an elderly border collie, bound to greet the visitor. The cosy bar of this house has one of the finest old open fireplaces in all Dorset.

The hosts restored it and scraped off twenty layers of paint. The building is 300 years old and has an inn sign which depicts the red rose on one side and a white rose on the other. It was designed by Lancastrian herald, Peter Gwynne Jones, who lives nearby.

This is an inn to my liking, specialising in home-made food.

This is a village pub in the old style, and on Mothering Sunday about 60 people sit down to lunch. A local organist, Anne Knobbs, sometimes entertains and there is a large skittle alley and private functions room.

An amusing notice is pinned above the bar referring to telephone calls. It reads that the landlord charges 50p for telling callers that you are not in; for 60p you have just left; 75p you have not been in; and for £1.00 he replies, 'Who?'.

An Eldridge Pope house.

THE SAILORS RETURN
East Chaldon

East Chaldon, also known as Chaldon Herring, is just off the main A352 road near Owermoigne.

'THEY turned the corner and saw *The Sailors Return* before them, standing alone a hundred yards or so from the village. It was a long low house, heavily thatched, with a post standing at one side to take a sign, but the sign was decayed and the frame stood empty'. So wrote author David Garnett 50 years ago in *'The Sailors Return'*, the story of new life being brought to a derelict inn, using the East Chaldon pub as background for the story.

In real life the situation has been repeated. For two years this inn, standing alone outside East Chaldon or Chaldon Herring, has been closed while the new owner sought planning permission. The enlarged premises will have the appearance of a lovely new/old inn once the paintwork has mellowed. Certainly, it would surprise the bedraggled smugglers who passed this way during its long years of existence.

Bill Davies is the manager of the free house which, on Sundays and Thursdays, features light music from a duo. But the accent is on a DIY effort and Bill invites customers to bring their own instruments to play. 'The piano is there if anyone wants to use it', encourages Bill.

It is hoped that the inn will become a local for regulars and residents from the villages and, with the farming folk in mind, there are hitching posts for equestrian callers.

A free house.

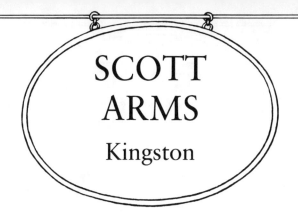

SCOTT ARMS

Kingston

At Kingston off the Corfe – Swanage road,
2½ miles out of Corfe.

DORSET explorers who love the Purbecks will be familiar with the *Scott Arms* at Kingston, but will need to come again to see the new Barn Bar with French windows opening on to the garden and one of the most beautiful and breathtaking views of Corfe's famous ruin.

The inn, dated 1650, takes its name from John Scott, First Earl of Eldon, a long serving Lord Chancellor, whose love story stirred hearts in the 18th century. In spite of parental opposition, he fled to Scotland with a rich banker's daughter, Bessie Surtees, and married her. He believed to his dying day that his wife was the perfect woman. They lived at nearby Encombe House.

Like so many Purbeck inns, the *Scott Arms* has a ghost . . . a lady who closes doors. There are several bars to cope with the busy summer trade, including a family room for the children.

On the walls of one bar is an interesting photographic record of cinema and television films made in the district including *The Mayor of Casterbridge, Hereward the Wake, Dr. Who, The Three Musketeers* and *Little Women*.

A Devenish house.

SHAVE CROSS INN
Marshwood Vale

The inn is in the heart of the Marshwood Vale about 5 miles north west of Bridport.

THE Marshwood Vale is one of West Dorset's treasures and is better known as the Vale of Blue Mists because, in early summer, it is carpeted by bluebells. At its heart, on the road from Marshwood to Bridport, is the *Shave Cross Inn* – easily missed because it hides behind an ancient hedge. Romantics will tell you that it was at this inn that Atte the Shaver lived, shaving the heads of pilgrims visiting the shrine of St. Wite in nearby Whitchurch Canonicorum. It is a thought to ponder on as you sit in the old world garden of this delightful thatched inn built of cob and flint, with 700 years of service, hoping to see the resident ghost . . . of course, a monk.

The more down-to-earth visitor will point out that the old English for shave is sceaga, a small copse or wood, and the cross refers to the road junction. I shall side with the romantics because this corner of Dorset is full of magic.

Here is a Dorset inn that comes near the top of my list of favourites. A garden wild and full of old world flowers (it won an award) and, in the corner, a little round house where long ago a cobbler worked. In the bar the sun streams through curtained casement windows and reflects in the scrubbed stone slabbed floor. The ancient beams bow over your head and, in winter, a great open fire roars in the brick inglenook.

But the high spot of this inn, hosted by a friendly young couple, is their Ploughman's Lunch. The farm butter melted on the cottage loaf hot from the oven, served with rich cheese and pickled onions bottled by 'Old Charlie' in the village. I felt so contented after a helping of Dorset Apple Cake, that I wondered if the pilgrims eating here before their last steps to the 13th century shrine of St. Wite, ever had dined so well.

Like old Atte, St. Wite is surrounded by legend. The 13th century church at Whitchurch Canonicorum is thought to be the only one with a patron saint buried on site, with the exception of Westminster Abbey.

St. Wite, or Candida, was a Breton princess in the 5th century. She was carried off by pirates but escaped when her virtue was assailed. Then, with her left hand chopped off, she walked back on the water to Brittany where she died. She was canonised in AD919 and her remains brought to Dorset.

A free house with a large range of beers and a skittle alley for private functions.

THE SHIP
Shaftesbury

On the hilltop near the Shaftesbury town centre.

WHEN you reach the *Ship Inn* perched on the Shaftesbury hilltop and looking out north over the neighbouring counties of Somerset and Wiltshire, you could believe that this very popular lunching place had been an inn since 1605, when it was built. In the cosy bar you can imagine buxom serving maids being jostled by drunken customers as they carried the foaming ale in jugs.

Truth is that it has only been an inn for 50 years and where you are sitting quenching your thirst, patients once sat waiting to consult Drs. A. Wilkinson and W.J. Harris. This was a doctors' surgery in the 1930s and the proof is hanging on the bar wall . . . the great brass plate bearing their names which used to adorn the front door. The hooded windows are a feature of the architecture of the early 17th century house.

The run out to Shaftesbury from the coast – about 32 miles – takes the visitor through some lovely Dorset villages including Tarrant Keyneston, Fontmell Magna and Iwerne Minster, and the road passes through the famous avenue of trees at Badbury Rings.

The farmer who planted them is said to have set up one for each day of the year. You will be surprised to find more than that number on one side alone.

———————

A Hall & Woodhouse house.

THE
SHIP INN
Langton Matravers

On the B3069 road out of Swanage.

THE 100 year old *Ship Inn* at Langton Matravers is a three-storey gaunt building on a Purbeck hilltop and has a macabre history. The inn was formerly in a smaller house, still adjoining it, and on a December night in 1878 the landlord, John Ball, and his incompatible wife, Mary, started a quarrel after closing time which resulted in his loading a gun with the intention of murdering her and taking his own life. Luckily, Mary made her escape through a window and John took the gun to himself and died alone in the public room. According to the law at that time, 'he was buried like a dog in unconsecrated ground.'

No fear of a repetition of this gruesome yarn at the new *Ship Inn*, built in 1884, because the bad publicity had made the old building unpopular. The warm and friendly welcome extended by today's hosts is the high spot of this rare Dorset inn, which still boasts a flagstone floor. They have lovingly created bars with stone hewn from the quarries around, and cleverly set old quarrying tools into the stonework to form a permanent museum.

The inn is also a base for the unusual game of shove-a-halfpenny on the long board – very different and more complex than the normal game. The polished slate is much longer than the traditional one and players score by getting coins into circles of different values at the top of the board. The game seems localised to the Purbecks in Dorset, where inns have a league. *The Ship* also has a tiddlywinks team. Bar snacks are served and local homemade Purbeck Pasties are much sought after.

A Whitbread house.

SHIP IN DISTRESS

Stanpit

Situated on the road from Purewell,
Christchurch to Mudeford Quay.

IF travellers pass the *Ship in Distress* at Stanpit, they miss an interesting location of Mudeford's historic past. It was a pub in the 17th century and Oliver Cromwell is said to have used it during the battle of Iford. In the 18th century, when smuggling was the business of many Christchurch folk, the inn was kept by the raven-haired widow, Hannah Siller. She was known as the Protective Angel of Smugglers. Through a channel from Mudeford, contraband was brought to a creek at the back of the inn for distribution to customers in the New Forest.

She was, however, crossed in love. A sea captain, one Billy Coombs, who owned the smuggling lugger John and Susannah, promised her marriage after his next trip and to retire and help her run the inn. She discoverd that such a promise was also made to another lady at Hamble. So scorned, she told the Preventers the time of his arrival at Mudeford and, after a battle, he was captured and hanged on Solent shore.

It is said that a former Earl of Malmesbury, then living at Hurn Court which was passed by the smugglers on their way across the heath to Kinson, was friendly to the 'Gentlemen of the Night' and, as they passed his house, he sat with his back to the window so that he could truthfully say that he had not seen them.

The inn takes its name from a shipwreck off Hengistbury Head from which Mudeford folk helped rescue survivors.

A Whitbread house.

THE
SHIP INN
Weymouth

*Situated on the harbourside a few yards from
the Town Bridge.*

A blue water bay with a curving sandy shore and a small but unique harbour are Weymouth's principal assets. The Dorset port, long a staging post for the steamers plying to the Channel Isles and Cherbourg, has never forgotten its Royal connections. Here it was that George III came to recuperate after illness and popularised sea bathing. The amusing story of his immersion, from the steps of a wheeled bathing hut, is part of the town's folklore. As lady attendants bounced him in the briny, a concealed band struck up the National Anthem.

On the harbourside, with windows offering a panoramic view of the docks, is the *Ship Inn,* at the end of one of the oldest terraces in the town. All the buildings are of Tudor and Stuart periods. In fact embedded in the walls of one old house is a cannonball fired from across the harbour during the Civil Wars. Generations of seamen have used this inn. In recent times it has been tastefully refurbished, retaining the old character. A large bonded warehouse adjoining has also been incorporated to provide an 86 seater Captains Bar and Restaurant, where fish dishes are a speciality.

The harbour is narrow and clinging to its sides are craft of all types and sizes. Smelly fishing drifters jostle with cruising yachts and pleasure boats. A cargo vessel may be sharing a berth with a Southampton Fire Tug in for repair and, in stormy weather, French fishing boats will line the quay two and three abreast. You will hear the tongues of many nations.

In the background is one of the country's largest lifeboats and where the Wey widens to meet the sea, the large cross-Channel ferry boats prepare for sailing. As you sit drinking, do not be surprised if you see a man walking in front of a train waving a red flag, because the boat train creeps right to the ferry's side and, in so doing, has to cross the main road which has no crossing gates. Sadly, the fleet of old paddle steamers, which used to moor right outside the inn for refuelling, have long departed. Each night black faced dockers carried the hundredweight sacks of coal across a plank from waiting trucks and dumped them in the holds. A ritual which drew crowds to the quayside. Gone also are the colourful Spritsail Thames Barges which brought sackloads of cement to the docks.

An outfall pipe from the breweries used to empty fluid into the Cove. It was a popular rendezvous for Weymouth swans who imbibed the foamy water and sailed uncertain courses up the harbour with their necks wobbling in an undignified manner.

A Hall & Woodhouse inn.

SILENT WOMAN
Cold Harbour Heath

*On the Wareham to Bere Regis road, three
miles out of Wareham.*

THE sign outside *The Silent Woman* inn at Cold Harbour,
between Wareham and Bere Regis on the Drax Estate, leaves
you in no doubt as to why it is so named. A headless woman
carries her head beneath her arm. The couplet underneath it reads:

> 'Since the Woman is Quiet,
> Let no man breed a riot.'

The lonely inn, formerly the *Angel,* is situated at the heart of all
that remains of Hardy's 'Blasted Heath', and in the story *The
Return of the Native* it is mentioned as 'The Quiet Woman Inn'.

Before the Second World War it was cloaked by the trees and
gave the appearance of a sinister hostel. Today much of the
woodland has been cleared and the inn, once an old farmhouse, is
bright and inviting.

A friendly family foursome make this pub popular with visitors
from miles around. The family has decorated the cosy bars with
military artifacts.

The Silent Woman has no live entertainment and there is a large
garden for children in summer.

A Hall & Woodhouse inn.

THE SMITHS ARMS
Godmanstone

Situated on the A352, eight miles north of Dorchester.

LEGEND tells us that King Charles II stopped at a blacksmith's forge in Godmanstone and requested of the smithy a glass of porter. 'I cannot oblige you Sire, as I have no licence,' he replied. Then said the King, 'From now on you have a licence to sell beer and porter.' It is doubtful whether the present landlord will oblige you with porter, but you can still buy a glass of fine ale in the forge where horses once stood to be shod, but where there is now a 20 ft. × 10 ft. bar – inviting, comfortable and cosy. Neatly thatched with a colourful sign depicting a smithy at work, the old *Smiths Arms* – built of mud and flint – claimed itself to be the smallest pub in England.

Another small pub at Bury St. Edmunds with the appropriate name of *The Nutshell* challenged Godmanstone's claim. In 1982 the rival landlords decided to settle the claim with a football match, and *The Nutshell* won. They returned to Godmanstone the following year for another match and won again. For some mysterious reason there have been no further return matches and *The Nutshell* is recorded in the *Guinness Book of Records* as the smallest inn.

If not the smallest, nothing can deter from the charm of the *Smiths Arms*. It stands on the banks of the little river Cerne where it follows its course to meet the bigger Dorset river Frome. There is a place for picnic tables where visitors can quaff their ale and watch little Muscovy ducks play around the river's banks.

A Devenish house.

THE SMUGGLERS
Osmington Mills

In a hill encircled hollow, beside the blue waters of Weymouth Bay, the Smugglers Inn at Osmington Mills awaits you. Turn off the main A353 at Osmington about 4 miles out of Weymouth. A narrow road leads you to Osmington Mills and its clifftop car park.

THERE is something romantic about the escapades of the oldtime smugglers, the infamous characters who risked all to bring home contraband – tea, spirits, tobacco, silk, soap and coffee. Like poachers, they were accepted as they waged their battles with the King's men. It is the modern smuggler, trading in hard drugs, who has vilified the ancient illicit trading. Gulliver, Hookey, and Slippery Rogers led their gangs locally, and the *Smugglers Inn* at Osmington was the base of Pierre Latour, the infamous 'French Peter'.

In the 18th century, the inn was known as the *Crown* and had its own brewery, later to become the *Picnic*. During the 1920s and 1930s it was famous for lobster teas. The shellfish were caught literally within yards of the inn. The lobsters are now scarcer and expensive, but sometimes they appear on the menu. Older residents will remember the Osmington Mills of their young days, because coach trips brought them there with the choice of lobster or strawberry teas.

It is claimed that the inn has been a social centre for this hamlet for 700 years.

Another name change and the inn became the *Smugglers*. In the older thatched portion, visitors can sit around the fireplace where generations of sailors, fishermen and smugglers have plotted and chatted and, through a haze of tobacco smoke, told their bawdy stories since the 13th century.

Long ago it was a kitchen and, during 'French Peter's' heyday, it is said that he sat and falsely plotted a consignment with the landlord, knowing full well that the local customs officer was hiding up the chimney. Gleefully, they kept stoking the fire until the officer,smoked out, had to disclose the fact that he was there. No doubt they all had a glass of brandy together.

The hosts of the *Smugglers* have attempted to revive the old tradition of the British inn, with good fare and a large variety of drinks. Ever 'ready to answer your call for a stoop of ale, a bite to eat and a bed for the night'.

From this location, where you can bathe and walk some of Dorset's loveliest cliffs, Constable painted his picture of Weymouth Bay when he was on his honeymoon.

Free House. Twenty different beers and ciders available.

THE SPYWAY

Askerswell

Askerswell is reached by a turning right off the Dorchester to Bridport main A35 road, ten miles beyond Dorchester.

IN a valley beneath the high road, which speeds traffic between Dorchester and the west, is as peaceful and unspoilt a village as you will find in all Dorset. Nestling by the massive heights of Eggardon Hill, Askerswell slumbers. A place heard of only when winter snow fills the valley. In keeping with this peace, the *Spyway Inn* has no music or fruit machines. Visitors can stand at the bar, decorated with horse brasses and rare tea cups, and look through windows, curtained in chintz, each side of the optics to take in a view of the rolling downs.

It is no wonder that visitors come here from as far afield as Bournemouth just for lunch. Home cooked pies, which can be eaten in any of the bars or children's room, are prepared by the popular hosts of this free house, 450 years old, and with smuggling connections. In 1745 it was an ale house called the *Three Horseshoes,* with a blacksmith's premises attached. In 1905 the stock in trade of the smithy was sold up ... the forge, bellows, anvil and tons of iron. The poster advertising the sale still hangs in the bar, and the buildings were incorporated into the inn which became known as the *Spyway* ... a name obviously connected with smuggling.

Children can play in the peaceful garden where ducks fuss around the pond – a soothing sound to disturb the silence.

A free house.

THE SQUARE & COMPASS
Worth Matravers

Off the B3069 road out of Swanage. Turn left at Acton shortly after passing Langton Matravers.

THE *Square & Compass* faces the sea high above the Purbeck coast at Worth Matravers, and has the appearance of a Devonshire village inn. At the end of a morning or evening walk along the clifftop between Dancing Ledge and Winspit, visitors climb through the valley to Worth to visit the quaint inn with whitewashed walls which glisten when the sun appears.

The Newman family have been mine hosts since 1907, and bearded Ray Newman is becoming as much of a character as his famous grandfather Charles – who reigned for 45 years. Celebrities came to argue with long faced landlord Charles. Augustus John was a regular and on the wall of the lounge bar is a cartoon of the famous painter, by Lowe. Many artists used Charles as a subject, among them Leon Heron whose cartoon of Charles chasing butterflies is also framed and hanging on the wall, which is covered with photographs and memorabilia.

Amongst the strange articles which cluster and adorn the walls is a giant crab encased, and Ray is at present preserving a 6lb lobster, 2 feet long, for display.

In winter, large open fires are a feature of this inn which, naturally, has smuggling connections. If you have heard your father talk of the pubs of yesteryear, then you will find the stone-flagged public bar, with scrubbed table tops and wooden settles, one of the finest examples in the county.

A Whitbread house

111

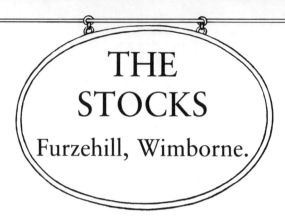

THE
STOCKS
Furzehill, Wimborne.

*Turn right off the B3078 road a mile or so
out of Wimborne and drive up the hill to
Furzehill.*

O N a cross roads atop a hill in Smugglers Lane at Furzehill,
a gruesome gibbet once stood on a windswept corner.
Today a direction sign spreads its arms at the site but
opposite is the *Stocks Inn,* as historic as its name suggests. The
original 16th century imprisoning stocks can be seen in the bar of
this 15th century building which was originally two cottages.

The *Stocks* complies with the picture postcard image of a Dorset
inn, crowned with uneven thatch and consequently a show place
for town based visitors who are brought here to savour a typical
Dorset hostelry. In winter, log fires burn merrily in the open bar's
great fireplace.

The inn has two floors of cellars and was a haunt of the
infamous Bournemouth smuggler, Gulliver. 'That man must have
had a bike' quipped the landlord, apologising for the fact that here
was another inn with Gulliver connections. There is supposed to
be a tunnel with entry onto Smugglers lane, and there was a
look-out tower at nearby Colehill where watchers kept an eye out
for approaching Preventive Officers.

The Stocks is only a few miles from Chalbury Hill, of which
historian Treves wrote: 'The air which sweeps over this hill is
pure and wholesome, while the view from its height is one of the
most fascinating in the County. To the east are the Ringwood
church, and the sweep of the New Forest. To the north Cranborne
Chase, and to the south, the water meadows of the Stour, the
Purbeck Hills and the Needles. The only blot on the landscape is
the nightmare Tower of Horton, built as an observatory it is now

happily falling into decay'. That was written in 1906. The tower is still with us, but the lovely hill range is a grand place to come to on a still summer's evening.

A Devenish House.

THE THATCHED HOUSE
Kinson

Situated in East Howe Lane at Kinson.

THE *Thatched House* has two claims to fame. It is a former gentleman's house roofed with neat thatch, one of the last remaining to remind us of Bournemouth's more elegant days. It is also only 150 yards from the site of the former home of Isaac Gulliver, the notorious smuggler chief. There was a public outcry in the 1950s when Gulliver's West Howe Lodge, purpose-built with hiding places and tunnels, was destroyed to make way for the housing estates which now dominate the area. Crenellations at roof level indicated its fortress-like quality. One secret room had its door ten feet up the chimney.

The nearby *Shrubberies,* built on Lord Wimborne's estate land in 1812, survived and – as a Grade 1 listed building – now gives shelter to its customers as the Thatched House inn. It has had very little internal alteration and there are only two bars. The hall and both front parlours were made into one large bar, but the fireplaces and roof decor leave the visitor in no doubt as to the original layout. A feature of the square fronted building is the original floor to ceiling length windows, with decorative mouldings.

Legend tells us that many of the houses in Kinson, a smuggling base, were linked with tunnels but no such escape route seems to have found its way to this house.

Personally I believe that most of these long tunnels, some supposedly reaching 3 miles to Branksome, were fictitious – in view of the sandy soil. It is probably more likely that the whole heath was dotted with deep wells opening on to concealing pits in which contraband could be quickly hidden, as approaching Preventivemen could be seen at a great distance on the open heath.

The Thatched House has no children's room but a lovely beer garden in summer. Concealed in the lanes of East Howe, it is mainly a 'locals' meeting place. In fact it prides itself on being a village pub, providing bar snacks.

An Eldridge Pope House.

THE THREE COMPASSES
Charminster

Situated in West Hill Road, Charminster, off the A352 road out of Dorchester to Sherborne.

THE *Three Compasses*, a gaunt brick building in the village of Charminster, hides behind properties along the main street and few visitors discover it. It is basically a locals' pub but nostalgia of a personal nature forces me to include it amongst my favourite inns.

Fifty years ago the *Three Compasses* was the monthly meeting place for journalists from all over Dorset who came to play on a magnificent skittle alley. It has changed little since those days when we quaffed strong ale and ate liberal portions of new cottage bread, farm butter, Blue Vinny cheese and raw onions: a delicacy the locals called a 'fum-bit', because you ate it squeezed between your palm and thumb.

Time has parted the friends who shared those happy evenings of bawdy stories and laughter. One became a barrister, another took holy orders and became a rural dean and some did not survive the Second World War. One thing is now missing from the inn of my memory – the old 'Sticker-up': a veteran in a flat cap with a heavy moustache, stained with decades of drinking and smoking, which hung over his lips like an untidy thatch. He would call the score and set up the pins after every throw for the price of an evening's free drinking. He is probably still shouting 'the backers up', in his rich Dorset dialect, in some Elysium hostelry to help the players in their mode of attack.

If you wish to call at this inn, drive up West Hill Road to the Square . . . a rough gravel car park shaded by a giant chestnut tree and bordered by a row of terraced houses on one side and a picturesque cottage on the other. The inn itself overlooks the Frome Valley and the course of the old Roman road between Dorchester and Ilchester.

A Devenish house.

THREE HORSESHOES

Burton Bradstock

On the B3157 coast road between Abbotsbury and Bridport.

LIKE most of the buildings in Burton Bradstock, the *Three Horseshoes* is built in the warm yellow coloured Ham stone which supports neatly thatched roofs. It became an inn during the late 17th century and today is hosted by a friendly family who make you welcome to this place of cosy bars. They ensure a warm atmosphere for people of all ages.

This is one of the Palmer houses featuring traditional Bridport real ale but, in spite of the old-world charm, you can see the cool, clean and clinical cellars where the beer is kept, through glass panels. Customers come to observe in the same way that sea-going folk inspected the massive shining pistons of the engines as they rose to collect drips of oil from the tiny wicks, when paddle steamers were popular.

The food is homemade and there is a family room and beer garden.

Cliff walks and beach are only 400 yards away, and nearby is an 18 hole golf course.

This lovely village is a labyrinth of narrow byways with such strange sounding names as Donkey Lane, Darby Lane and Shadrick.

It is three miles from Bridport, and where Bournemouth smuggler, Isaac Gulliver, used the beaches for his western connection.

A Palmer house.

THE THREE HORSESHOES
Powerstock

Powerstock is five miles north east out of Bridport on the Bridport to Maiden Newton road.

IN the lush green hills which climb away from the coast, Powerstock is a village of cottages dotted over the hills, and has a valley through which flows a glittering brook. King Athelstan had a palace here a long time ago, but all that is left is a green mound.

In the heart of the village, near the Norman church, is the 300 year old *Three Horseshoes Inn* – rebuilt after a fire at the turn of the century. Now a Victorian inn where the landlord and his wife welcome you, and have a reputation for their cooking.

In spite of the peaceful surroundings, Powerstock is a working village and if you prolong your stay at the inn, you will watch the cows march down the main street at milking time.

The inn has a pine panelled dining room, restored by removing layers of paint, wallpapers and hardboard. As well as traditional beers, scrumpy is sold on draught.

After refreshment at the inn, drive up the lonely narrow road which seems to be endless, but leads to the height of ancient Eggardon Hill with its lines of strong green ramparts. It is at 820 feet and looks out over miles of dale, woods and hedgerows.

The *Three Horseshoes* played a prominent part in a strange scandal in the 1830s. Suspicions were roused when two parishioners, John Hounsell and Elizabeth Gale, asked for their banns of marriage to be read. The vicar was suspicious because John's wife had died the previous November at their nearby Nettlecombe home after being nursed by Elizabeth, whose husband had died shortly before the approach for the banns to be read. The Rev. George Cookson reported the situation to the police and the two bodies were exhumed and placed in the church. The altar was used as a slab to perform the post mortem, and it took weeks to clear up the mess and make the church fit for use again. The examination disclosed that John Hounsell's wife contained enough arsenic to kill half a dozen people, and he was charged and sent for trial at Dorchester. To everyone's surprise, he was acquitted due to insufficient evidence as to how the arsenic came to be in the body. The banns of John Hounsell and Elizabeth Gale were duly called on three occasions in 1839 but, strangely, there is no record in the church of their marriage. They just disappeared.

A Palmers house.

THE TIGERS HEAD
Rampisham

Off the A356 road from Dorchester to Crewkerne, near the tall masts of the BBC Relay Station.

THAT great Dorset historian, Sir Frederick Treves, describes Rampisham as one of the most beautiful villages in Dorset. A place of old thatched cottages with a tiny creeper-covered inn of great antiquity and singularly low stature bearing the ferocious title of the Tigers Head.

He was describing the inn during its thatched days, but it was rebuilt in 1915. Although I have heard of other Tiger inns, this is the only Tiger's Head I have encountered, and no one seems to know how it gets its name.

It is a friendly inn and, if you stay the night, you have a choice of four posters and brass bedsteads. Children can meet Gladys the bulldog in the children's room, and there are ducks in the beer garden.

The village really is enchanting, standing in a valley of trees with a stream which crosses the road over a shallow ford outside the thatched village post office.

———————————

A free house.

TURKS HEAD

Chickerell

The village of Chickerell is on the B3157 road 3 miles out of Weymouth.

CHICKERELL hides just off the main coast road to Abbotsbury, three miles out of Weymouth. Old timers will tell you that it is not really a village, but – in the dim past – a settlement for law breakers, and monks journeying from Abbotsbury called there to give them Absolution. Before I get deeper in trouble, I hasten to add that Chickerell today is a very law abiding place, neatly and pleasantly growing around the *Turks Head* – an inn of antiquity and charm.

The restaurant buildings are dated 1769 but the adjoining inn is much older. Situated near the coast and adjoining village of Fleet with smuggling connections, the *Turks Head* was frequently visited by the notorious 'Gentlemen of the Night'. Mine hosts are Tom and Heather Williams who hail from the picturesque Lleyn Peninsula in North Wales – my own favourite part of the British Isles outside Dorset.

Their food is mouth-watering and the pub is a meeting place for Sunday lunch parties. Children are allowed in the restaurant and Friday night is dinner dance night. Groups sometimes appear and the inn, with a large spacious bar, has a skittle alley.

A Devenish house.

TRUE LOVERS KNOT

Tarrant Keyneston

*On the main Bradbury Rings road from
Wimborne to Blandford.*

WHETHER you approach Tarrant Keyneston from the north or south, it is a long downhill run to the village in the valley, known as the fastest High Street in the west, and clustered around a crossroads where the Bournemouth to Blandford road crosses the twisting narrow road which follows the course of the little river Tarrant on its ramble to the Stour.

Here, an old school on one corner and the village shop on another face the 250 year-old inn with the strange name of the *True Lovers Knot*.

Why it is so named is a mystery, but many stories are told concerning the three looped knot. Ever the romantic, I like the version told me by the licensee. It appears that many years ago the then landlord's daughter became pregnant but she would not name the father, saying that it could be one of three village lads. The father invited all three to the inn, got them drunk and hanged the three of them.

If the exterior of the Hall and Woodhouse inn – like other buildings on the crossroads – has altered little over the years, the interior has been redesigned into bars with old world charm.

Precede your visit to the *True Lovers* with a drive up the Tarrant valley and enjoy the quaint villages of Gunville, Monkton, Launceston, Rawston and Rushton. The journey is only a few miles and you will be rewarded with glimpses of beautiful Dorset downland.

A Hall & Woodhouse inn.

125

THE WELD ARMS
Lulworth

*Lulworth is on the B3070, off the main
A352 out of Wareham.*

THE little thatched hamlet of East Lulworth, with cottages clustered around the ruined castle, has a cosy inn which bears the Weld family coat of arms on its sign, because Lulworth is the home of the Welds who first came in 1641 and are still here.

In this very English rural atmosphere, the visitor may think it odd that the landlord is an adventuring ocean-going yachtsman who has taken part in two solo transatlantic races, and competed twice in Round Britain events. He is not so out of place because a previous lord of the manor was Joseph Weld who, in the middle of the last century, raced the giant cutter Alarm at Cowes.

The bars are decorated with yachting memorabilia and club burgees. The inn has three bars and provides travellers with exciting menus which include whole prawns and scallops.

There is accommodation for children and a garden for the warm days of summer. *Weld Arms* barbecues will be popular when the weather is right.

Although Lulworth was the base of a particularly rough set of smugglers, there is no record of activity at the inn, but maidservants of the castle used to signal with candles high up in the towers when Preventivemen were about. In fact, this smuggling connection with the Weld's castle spanned nearly all of the 18th century.

A Devenish house, leased to them by the Weld Estate.

WHITE HART
Bishops Caundle

*Bishops Caundle is on the A3030 road
between Sherborne and Sturminster Newton,
about 8 miles from Sherborne.*

BISHOPS Caundle has a musical sounding name, Caundle being a range of hills owned by the Bishop of Sarum in the 13th century. But few visitors would rate the village as a sightseeing attraction – in spite of the cosy cottages deep in thatch which straggle through this vale of rich pastures.

My friend, the late Pat Palmer, author of *What's In a Name,* said solemnly as we stood 'neath the tower of the 500 year old church: 'Old men stood on this same spot who had seen the hail of arrows at Agincourt.'

'I hope it was on a sunnier day', I retorted, much to his disgust.

Dorset dialect poet, William Barnes, also spent happy hours 'neath the old dun tower and recorded coming to Caundle for a feast day to celebrate the victory at Waterloo.

> 'At Peace Day, who but we should goo
> To Caundle for an hour or two.
> . . . In Caundle for a day at least
> You woudden vind a scowlen feace,
> Or dumpy heart in all the pleace.'

He told of the merry faces of the throng and garlands and wreaths on every side, and coloured flags a fluttering high, and how they came through the high barn doors to dine on English fare.

Visitors are once again coming to Bishops Caundle for the fare. The 16th century White Hart did not have the welcoming exterior of a village inn for many years. 'Let's press on', we used to say in passing, 'and get a drink in Sherborne'.

However, in the 1980s, the White Hart has become a social centre to which people flock from as far away as Bournemouth for the enjoyment of village inn atmosphere, and to sample the wide range of homemade cooking. Such is its fame that it was voted 'Top Badger Inn' out of 164 Hall & Woodhouse houses in 1965.

The young hosts have the backing of villagers who give their time to help serve at this popular cosy inn with low ceilings and beams, and it is a rule that no one leaves the White Hart without a member of staff bidding them farewell. That goes for those who leave by car or those who use the ancient mounting block at the front door to assist them in getting astride their horses.

That mounting block is one of the old touches of the inn. Where the lounge bar is now situated was once the place where monks brewed their beer for a nearby monastery. In the building's long history, it has served as court house for the infamous Judge Jeffreys and recently a hide was discovered in the roof during alterations.

Hall & Woodhouse.

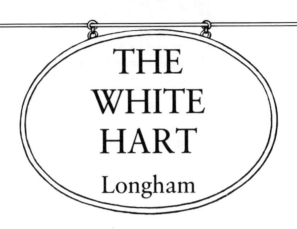

THE WHITE HART
Longham

*On the main A348 road and at the heart of
the village of Longham.*

IT must be no surprise that the infamous Bournemouth smuggling chief, Isaac Gulliver, features in so many Dorset inns. As
he became more prosperous and opened his western connection
using routes from the coast of Bridport and Lyme to supply the
wealthy customers in the Bath area, his men needed the cover of
many hostelries. However, we are asked to believe that the White
Hart at Longham was one of his more respectable business
ventures. Ten years previously, he had married Elizabeth Beale –
daughter of the landlord of the Blacksmith's Arms at Thorney
Down – and, following his father-in-law as landlord, displayed his
wry sense of humour by renaming the pub *The King's Arms,*
because of his 'loyalty to the Crown'!

If his interest in the *White Hart,* which he came to in 1778, was
legitimate, it was also noticeable that it was close to the Bournemouth beaches where his 15 luggers constantly called. He left the
inn in 1780 to live in his purpose-built house at Kinson.

Long ago the famous artist, Augustus John, was a visitor to the
inn with his friend, a local farmer. This gentleman objected to
racing aircraft from the old aerodrome at Northbourne using the
village as a turning point and took a shotgun to one of the planes
as it passed over. The gun was on display at the *White Hart* for
many years.

The inn no longer has the cosy little bars of John's day but has
been opened out into one long bar with log fires at each end.

It is said that early in the last century the toll road from
Winchester to Poole ended nearby and such was the pub's

reputation for drunkenness and violence that the Temperance authorities erected a coffee house at the site of the former Lowes store on the present Longham roundabout, so that disembarking passengers from the stage coaches would not have to become involved with the inn.

The *White Hart* has a beer garden and duos entertain on Saturday nights.

It is supposed to have a ghost, but I believe that 'she' is the mischievous creation of a former landlord, who I know well.

_____

A Hall & Woodhouse inn.

WHITE HART
Sturminster Newton

Over the bridge off the Blandford to Sherborne road, the White Hart is on the left in the Square.

STURMINSTER Newton, little Minster town on the banks of the twisting Stour, lives in the past. The bridge which enables you to cross the river and climb into the ancient square, warns that you will be deported if you damage it. But the busy factory town of 200 years ago now only comes to life on market day.

The *White Hart,* with dormer windows deep set into the thatch, is one of the inns frequented by farming folk. It overlooks the remains of the old Cross, with well-worn steps on which the Dorset poet, William Barnes, sat as a child. It forms a grandstand for those who wish to linger and watch the traffic pass through the narrow streets.

Like many old inns today, the several bars of the *White Hart* are now one. but it is tastefully modernised and decorated in old world style with open fireplaces.

At this 18th century coaching inn, a notice on the wall gives its date as 1707.

The inn boasts a skittle alley and a good menu.

A car-run north from Bournemouth or Poole should be broken by visiting the picturesque mills of Fiddleford and Sturminster. Both are near the inn and the latter is still working.

I have memories of a Christmas Eve spent in the bar of the *White Hart*. Lingering snow was clinging to the thatched buildings in the Square and, around the Cross, well-wrapped schoolchildren – some carrying oil lamps on poles – were grouped to sing carols.

The scene was reminiscent of a Dickensian Christmas card. In the cosy atmosphere of the *White Hart,* events were taking place which give an insight into the happy life style of this Minster town.

The bar was crowded and, one by one, the local tradesmen dropped in, dressed in the garb of their various trades, to entertain. The butcher in apron and straw hat sang a song. Another staged a mock 'drunken' fight with the burly blacksmith – a hilarious battle which drew rounds of applause. When it came to my turn, I told a joke which I have no intention of repeating here!

A Hall & Woodhouse Badger house.

THE WINYARDS GAP INN

Cheddington

Winyards Gap is on the Dorset/Somerset border on the A356 road between Crewkerne and Maiden Newton.

THERE have been many inns at Winyards Gap at Cheddington, 770 feet high on the chalk hills of West Dorset, the famous cutting, tucked beneath an ancient earthwork. From here the road twists rapidly downhill to cross the border into Somerset. Armies have marched past, as well as market bound sheep and cattle. Kettle drums beat out a rhythm as King Charles I led his troops through the Gap in 1644, and the innkeeper and customers came out to watch. The inn also knew of smuggling activity – it was not far from the infamous Isaac Gulliver's western smuggling connection, and highwaymen accosted many a traveller at this lonely place.

It was a famous 18th century court case concerning a wayward eighteen year old girl's holiday which brought Winyards Gap more recent fame.

The girl, Elizabeth Canning, in service in London, went missing for a month on what we must believe was an extended naughty weekend. Arriving home in a sorry and bedraggled state, she claimed that a gypsy called Mary Squires and a brothel keeper, Susannah Wells, had kept her virtually a prisoner in a house for immoral purposes. It was Mary Squires' alibi that at the time in question she was staying at the *Winyard's Gap Inn* in Dorset, but she was convicted and sentenced to death. The Lord Mayor of London, Sir Crispin Gascoyne, who was also the Master of the Brewers Company, came to Dorset, checked her story and earned her a pardon. The naughty Elizabeth Canning was sentenced for perjury and sent to a penal colony for seven years.

The trees have been cleared from the Gap to give views of the Mendips, Quantocks and Glastonbury Tor from terraces and lawns which now front the enlarged Inn, with large comfortable bars, facilities for handicapped visitors, and a children's and function room. All overlook the Somerset countryside. Tourists flock through the Gap in the 1980s and, stopping at the inn, enjoy home-cooked food, such as Beef Carbonnade cooked in Bass.

On a hillock behind the inn, on land given as a memorial to the 43rd Wessex Division of the Dorsetshire Regiment, stands a replica of the memorial on Hill 112 at Caen, Normandy, with which the 43rd will be forever associated.

A free house featuring Bass and Eldridge Pope Ales.

THE
WISE
MAN
West Stafford

Turn off the A35 near Dorchester on the
road marked Higher and Lower
Bockhampton, the villages of Hardy's
childhood. Continue South to West Stafford
and the Wise Man.

O N a sunny winter morning I lost my way in the lanes which weave through Thomas Hardy's storyland, the dour background to many of his sad stories, when by accident I came to a crossroad and a thatched pub.

If you like the old style inn which dispenses a warm welcome as well as excellent ale, then you will be happy at the *Wise Man*, at West Stafford, near Dorchester.

This hostelry, hosted by a charming family, not only welcomes your dog but many of the locals keep a dog bowl at the inn.

The 400 year old thatched building was once a village shop and off-licence. Now the Village Parlour, the Lounge and the Restaurant all display a magnificent show of Toby Jugs hanging from the ceiling as well as cases of antique pipes.

Richard and Helen Lipsett with son Shaun are the hosts. Helen, a cordon bleu cook, specialises in beef in Guinness, ham stews and fudge cakes.

Morris Men sometimes add a touch of colour to the Devenish Inn which bears this strange poem on a plaque on the outside wall. . .

'I trust no wise man will condemn
A cup of genuine now and then
When you are faint your spirits low

Your string relaxed twill bend your bow
Brace your drumhead and make you tight
Wind up your watch and put you right
But then again the two much't use
Of all strong liquors is the abuse
Tis liquid makes the solid loose
The texture and whole frame destroys
But health lies in the equipoise'.

It has been said that Thomas Hardy was the author. This is
doubtful; in fact Hardy died before the *Wise Man* became an inn.

A Devenish House.

THE WORLDS END

Almer

Situated on the A31 road about six miles out of Wimborne.

THE *Worlds End Inn* at Almer is one of the oldest pubs in Dorset. It dates back to 1589 and holds the oldest beer licence issued in the county. Before the Second World War it was a small sparsely decorated pub standing in a short cul-de-sac lane. Visitors, attracted by the inn's strange name, were not made very welcome and locals mulled their ale over a smoky open fire.

Today it is a leading social centre, much enlarged, and attracts visitors in hordes who flock to the Almer inn like wasps around a jam pot. Structural beams in the old part of the inn include ships' timbers reputed to have come from vessels involved with the Spanish Armada. It was the haunt of smugglers and the list of landlords has been traced back to 1740. The old pub also held a licence for 'gilbert and baker' – giving it the right to stage auctions and bake bread. The bread oven is still on show, and a high-wayman's bolt hole runs parallel to the chimney, providing a quick getaway for anyone in trouble.

A lot of the inn's fame arises from the misconception that Field Marshal Montgomery planned the D-Day invasion in this thatched inn. A post war landlord cashed in on this legend and even set up a table and chair in the bar, claiming them to be Monty's. By the late 1960s the story had snowballed and people were saying how Eisenhower, Churchill and Montgomery and others were sitting on the pub lawn in 1944 planning the D-Day invasion.

A new landlord, troubled that visitors kept insisting on sleeping in Monty's room, decided to clear up the matter. He wrote to

Monty who replied that he had never stayed at the inn, but once had lunch there in 1940 when he returned from Dunkirk. At the time he was commanding 5 Corps, responsible for the defence of Hampshire and Dorset should Hitler invade.

Today the inn features naval photographs and memorabilia given by sailors who call when journeying between Portsmouth and Plymouth. But most noted is Monty's letter telling how he lunched there.

A Hall & Woodhouse inn.

WORLDS END — ALMER.

YE OLDE STARRE INNE

Christchurch

Situated on the main Christchurch to Purewell road just past the bridges over the Avon.

WHEN you pass Ye Olde Starre Inne on the Christchurch to Purewell road you get the impression of a very old rambling inn, yet only a very small portion of it is genuinely 17th century.

Over the years the ancient heart of the building spread wings incorporating adjacent buildings, garden and outhouses to create three large bars. When you are inside there is little chance of telling the difference between the old beams and the fake.

Ships' lanterns and nautical brasswork create the seafaring atmosphere in this former smugglers' inn. The pub is a centre for young people. On Mondays live music is provided by duos.

Fish is, naturally, prominent on the menu of hot and cold bar meals, and Scotch beef steaks are a speciality.

Christchurch is a compact little town with all its historic buildings, and the beautiful Priory – all within a few hundred yards of Ye Olde Starre Inne. The waterfront is formed by the meeting of the Hampshire Avon and the Dorset Stour which, from here, flow together into Christchurch Bay.

A Free House.

Index

Square & Compass, Worth Matravers

Acknowledgements

I would like to thank the *Evening Echo*, Bournemouth. The book is based on the feature series 'Far from the Madding Crowd' and 'Inn and Around' and the kind co-operation of the Editor, Mr. W.M. Hill and General Manager, Mr. M. Emsley, made the book possible. *Echo* artist John Baker was not only responsible for the colourful cover but also the excellent inn illustrations, except some of the Hall & Woodhouse inns portrayed by Jacquelyn Evans, Jacquelyn Fortnam and Clayton Hoyle.

Thanks also to the Brewery P.R. Officials, Brian Miller of Hall & Woodhouse, Andrew Coop of Devenish and Douglas Pratt of Eldridge Pope and all those friendly hosts and hostesses who made the research of this book a pleasurable experience.

Di Pestell once again made the manuscript presentable and has already started her own inn exploration.

Finally I must thank Canon W.G. Rowley of Bridport who with me re-visited some of our haunts of 50 years ago, making a nostalgic journey around some of the rare inns of Dorset.

Harry Ashley